MINISTRY SOLUTIONS

264

Great

OUTREACH
IDEAS

For Individual Christians
and for Churches

JOEL D. HECK
editor

SAINT LOUIS

Contents

Preface

Many people who read this book will be looking for that perfect method—the one that the church has been missing for decades, no, make that centuries, but which, if implemented, will result in rapid growth for any church that tries it. Those readers will be disappointed. There is no such cure-all.

Please don't open this book looking for "buses, badges, balloons, and baloney." Instead look at two other things: first, God's strong Word and your church's ministry. Second, look at your community to understand its unique needs and at a book like this for ideas to equip the saints (Eph. 4:11–12) of your church to carry that Word to the people in your community.

A look at God's strong Word will equip you with the truths you must convey in order for people to acknowledge their sin, their need for a Savior, and the gracious provision for their salvation in the person and work of Jesus Christ.

A look at your church's ministry will tell you what you are or are not doing. What sort of delivery system do you have for getting the message of the Gospel out? Who is doing this work? How many people are involved, both on the frontlines (e.g., making calls on newcomers in the community) and behind the scenes (e.g., praying, sending copies of local newspaper clippings to those who are featured, correcting Bible correspondence lessons)?

A look at your community will tell you some of its needs. Speak to the leaders in local government, business, industry, churches, and schools. Find out what needs they perceive and how your church can meet them.

A look at this book may be unnecessary if you take a good, long look at God's Word, your ministry, and your community.

If, however, you still need some practical ideas for implementation—some methods for delivering the message—then read on.

Many people have supplied the great outreach ideas included in this book. Some, those who shared their ideas directly with the editor, are named. Many others, those whose ideas have become part of the general corpus of outreach theology and practice, cannot be thanked by name. Nevertheless, to every direct or indirect contributor we owe our gratitude. Surely "we are surrounded by such a great cloud of witnesses" (Heb. 12:1). A significant number of these outreach ideas have appeared in the periodical *Evangelism,* in particular in its IDEA BANK column.

Joel D. Heck, Editor

How to Use This Book

Don't read this book in one sitting, please! Don't even try. But do read this book one idea at a time. If you serve on your congregation's evangelism committee, put one or two ideas on your agenda each month. Share the ideas and discuss the possibilities of implementing them. Better yet, buy a copy of the book for every member of the committee. But take the ideas one or two at a time, lest you choke on the amount of material. "A journey of a thousand miles begins with the first step."

Don't expect all known ideas about outreach and evangelism to appear in these pages. They wouldn't fit in a book 10 times this size! The editor made some choices based on quality, impact, and usefulness, concentrating on ideas that have appeared in the past 10 years. A few books and program materials have been listed. If you know of additional outreach ideas, please send them to the editor, and let him learn from you.

This book is a digest of many ideas, not a complete explanation of each idea. If you need more information, you are invited to contact the people or organizations listed on the following pages, not the editor or the publisher. Following many specific ideas, in parentheses, are the names of the individuals or organizations that shared them. You will find their full addresses in the back of the book.

Part 1

Great Ideas for Individual Christians

General Concepts Individuals Can Use to Reach Out

Conversation

The Q-L-T Method. To start a conversation, keep it going, and move it toward a witness situation, try the Q-L-T method:

Question: Ask questions about the person. If the person is a stranger, ask about where they live, what they do, their family, etc. If the person is an acquaintance, ask about their recent activities or their opinions about current issues.

Listen: After asking some questions, take time to listen. Careful listening can communicate concern and earn the right to share thoughts.

Tell: Tell your experiences and opinions, especially as they reflect your faith in Jesus Christ. (Erwin J. Kolb)

The C-C-F Method. Most conversations wander aimlessly from subject to subject, including the weather, sports, and politics. Rarely do they include church or faith in Jesus Christ. The C-C-F method shows you how to include those topics!

Chitchat: Most conversations need to start with chitchat. This warms the relationship and opens lines of communication.

Church: After chitchatting for a time, move the conversation toward a discussion of faith by using a transition step, talking about church. Try the Q-L-T method, above (Question-Listen-Tell). Ask about church background, church involvement, church news, or opinions about the church, and then, listen.

Faith: From talking church, it is an easy step to talking faith, using Q-L-T. Ask what their church says about some subject, what they believe about life after death, etc. (Erwin J. Kolb)

Speculate. I've usually found that people don't want to say that they believe this or that, so I try to get them to speculate by asking a penetrating question. "If there is no 'maybe' and you had to choose between one or another, would you say that there's life after death or not?" Or, "Would you say that God interests Himself in the affairs of people or not?" It's very important to ask people not to qualify their answers so they will think on their own. (Moishe Rosen)

Leading Questions. Some who have the gift of evangelism use leading questions to open the door for sharing the Gospel. After introductory remarks, by asking questions to get a person talking about himself or herself, the Christian can often see a sharing opportunity.

For example, state that you hate religiosity or churchianity, but that you are sold on real Christianity. One of Christ's chief messages was this: "Do you want to be made well or whole?" That's vastly different from "getting religion," and it communicates in a language that the unbeliever can understand. Often people will ask what you mean. That is the time to offer brochures that address the needs they have. (Dick Innes)

Talking Church. Yes, it's true that inviting someone to your church is not witnessing per se. It's also true that talking about your church or its programs or pastor is not witnessing. However, the subject of church is one of the best transitions from conversation about secular matters to conversation about spiritual matters.

You can be talking about anything—the weather, sports,

current events, politics—and inject a comment like this: "By the way, I've never asked you if you have a church home. Do you attend somewhere?" The reply you get from a friend or neighbor will invariably be cordial. The answer will dictate how you follow up.

How Americans Think. The Gallup organization has identified two strong undercurrents in American society: (1) the search for meaning in life, probably because of the shallowness of modern life, and the rejection of materialism and (2) the search for meaningful relationships to alleviate the problem of loneliness. People who capitalize on the latter will make friends with non-Christians, and they will address the former in conversation (*Net Results,* June 1990, p. 2).

Friendship (See Also Lifestyle, Below)

The Bridge of Friendship. You will read a lot about the importance of friendship in those portions of this book that deal with Friendship Sunday, hospitality, lifestyle evangelism, marketplace, and other subjects. Friendship is the bridge across which the Gospel most frequently travels.

Life Issues. Stay tuned to issues and events in the lives of your friends—Baptisms, birthdays, graduations, etc. Respond to them personally or with cards. (Jerry White)

Keep in Touch. Don't lose communication with your non-Christian friends. Keep in touch with high school classmates, college classmates, neighbors, etc., even for decades. (Jerry White)

Hospitality

Your Children's Friends. In today's society knowing our children's friends has become necessary for the safety of our children. An even better reason for knowing our children's friends is the opportunity to share Jesus with them.

Young people often look for a place to be and for things to do. Open your home to your children and their friends for that purpose. Those who most miss the things you have to offer will be among your best prospects. In the process you and your children will have many opportunities to witness, to invite friends to events at church, to bring them to worship.

Have People Over. Having people over is no longer common in America. There are still parties, but a party is not like having people over for low-key friendly talk during a relaxed evening.

Have one or two families over at most. Make your visitors comfortable, the food simple. Use paper plates if you wish. During such an evening, friendly sharing can occur. It can also be a time when you can share your faith. Make it a point to do at least three things: relax, encourage repeat visits (your perfect meal and spotless house may discourage return invitations), and be natural. Don't push Jesus. Just be yourself and talk about Him as you would with your family and Christian friends.

Bible Study. Start a "Your Home a Lighthouse" Bible study in your neighborhood. Use *Your Home a Lighthouse,* by Bob and Betty Jacks, NavPress, which is also available in video format. (Jerry White) See also the resources from the organization Neighborhood Bible Studies (listed under "Organizations" later in the book).

Marketplace

Being Available. Since I do not have the gift of personal evangelism and all of my training is in confrontational evangelism, I became increasingly frustrated with my witness for Christ. I felt very threatened and uncomfortable with what I consider "hard-sell" evangelism. When I tried to share my faith, I felt embarrassed and am certain my listeners did too. If the truth were known, I probably did more to turn people from Christ than I ever did to bring them to Him. I never won anybody to Christ this way. Furthermore, whenever I tried confrontational evangelism, I felt like David trying to wear Saul's armor. It just didn't fit.

This is not to say that there is not a time and place for confrontational evangelism. There is, when the listener is ready to hear the plan of salvation and when the witness has the gift of personal or confrontational evangelism. However, trying to do something for which one is not gifted can readily lead to a deep sense of failure and withdrawal from any form of evangelism.

There came a time when I finally threw "Saul's armor" away. I was very frustrated with confrontational evangelism and was constantly feeling guilty because I wasn't witnessing more. In utter frustration I told God I hated witnessing and was quitting!

What I actually meant was that I hated buttonholing people and witnessing out of a sense of duty or, even worse, out of a sense of guilt. Nevertheless, I continued my prayer by saying, "However, God, if you want to use me to get the Gospel out, I'm available. But you'll have to do it through me because I'm just too scared."

Within a few hours I was on an airplane sitting by myself reading a book about Christ's return. Another passenger sat down beside me, introduced himself, and asked what I was reading. "It's a book about Jesus Christ's return to earth," I answered.

He asked, "Do you believe Christ is coming back again?"

I replied, "Yes, I do."

"Would you tell me all about it?" he quite enthusiastically asked.

Now, I love witnessing like that. I had told God I was available, and everything about this conversation flowed naturally.

As a result, for the last 15 years or so, every morning, I have prayed, "God, I'm available today. Please make me usable and help me today to be as Christ to my family, to someone in need, and in some way to every life I touch." God has given me many opportunities to talk about my faith in a very natural and easy way. (Dick Innes)

Workplace. In the workplace Christians usually have the opportunity to meet and talk with people.

Break times provide opportunities to discuss the weather, solve world problems, talk about family events, and cheer on the local team. "I did" or "This happened to me" commonly introduce conversations that often are personal and sometimes have substance.

Although talk about religion may not be allowed, solving problems is common to workplace conversations. Christians have the opportunity to share how Jesus solves many of our problems. We can mention quite naturally our spiritual life as a source of strength.

An Open Bible. Put your Bible on your desk at work. That could dare people to ask. Keep a give-away, spare Bible (modern translation) in a drawer. You may want to include in it a guide to selected verses. (Kent R. Hunter)

Meeting a Need

Your Own Needs Open Doors. Prayerfully and thoughtfully identify areas where you have failed (lost a job, ruined a marriage, betrayed a trust, etc.), sinned (abused alcohol or drugs, stolen something, etc.), or been deeply hurt (death of a child or spouse, lies told about you, etc.). Ask God to help you, when it is appropriate, to admit your need as you reach out to an unbeliever who is suffering in a similar way.

People are often open to the Gospel when they are hurting, when they have failed, or when they are devastated by their sins. If they can see that the love of Christ has healed me, then they may trust Christ in their weakness. See 2 Cor. 12:9–10 and Matt. 9:12–13. (Lyle W. Dorsett)

Neutral Territory. One of the advantages of meeting needs is that this usually occurs on neutral territory away from church property. (Dick Innes)

Seminars on Needs. Another way to meet needs is to offer seminars or workshops that address the needs of people who are hurting, recovering, or in need of a support group.

Dick Innes has conducted seminars on "Loving and Understanding People," that have brought in non-Christians, several of whom have become Christians.

Storytelling

Most People Love Stories. Storytelling can be fun, serious, educational, or boring. To tell a story well, tell it often to imprint it on your memory, and know when to tell it to make the most powerful impact.

You can witness to the love of God in Jesus Christ through stories. Since Jesus is central to the life of the Christian, our own stories will include a witness to what God has done in our lives. Follow these simple guidelines:

1. *Earn the right to tell your story:* The good storyteller knows the audience. Ask questions. Respond to the comments or questions of the persons with whom you are sharing.
2. *Choose a story that fits:* Forcing a story, artificially, can quickly end a conversation. By listening well, you can select a story to meet a need in the other person's life. For example, "Yes, I feel frustrated too when my life gets hectic. I was once so tired I slept 20 hours straight ..." (By the way, this is an excellent opening to tell about the peace that Jesus brings to your life.)
3. *Just tell the story:* When someone spends a lot of time telling you how funny their story is going to be, you want to say, "If it is really funny, JUST TELL IT." Don't preach. Don't apologize. Don't set up. Simply tell about your experience. Because you are a Christian, Christ will be a part of many experiences. Don't explain. A good story stands on its own. The person with whom you are sharing will respond. Answer only the questions the person asks.
4. *Practice:* During your family devotions (with your family's permission), tell your story of what Jesus has done in your life.

15

Times of Transition

At about 10 o'clock at night my telephone rang. A concerned member said, "Pastor, I have a very urgent request. Could you go down to the hospital tonight and see a very dear friend of mine? He is not a Christian, and he had a terrible experience this morning. They took him down to surgery and gave him a sedative injection, and his heart stopped. They got it started again but delayed the surgery. Tomorrow morning they will try it again. I tried to share my faith with him, but he really needs help."

A few minutes later I walked into his darkened room. He was still awake, visibly concerned about the next day. I introduced myself and told him that his friend had shared with me what had happened. I had come at this late hour because I really wanted to be helpful. I assured him that it was not necessary to go into the operating room alone. God, who had made him and given him everything he had, would gladly go with him!

One thing was urgent—that he be at peace with God. We talked about what Jesus went through to purchase our forgiveness and how He wanted everyone on earth to receive it. I wrapped it all up by saying, "Let's join in a prayer asking for His forgiveness and asking Him to guide the surgeon's hand and stay with you with His healing presence." He gladly agreed, and we prayed. Afterward he said, "Pastor, if I ever get out of this place alive, the first place I'll come will be to your church."

I had heard this promise before. However, this time it was genuine. A few weeks later this man sat in a church pew. Several months later he and his wife knelt at the altar and spoke their confirmation vows. Since then several members of their family have followed their example.

I had discovered something valuable. People don't usually argue about having forgiveness the night before surgery. They have already been crushed by the Law and are ready for the comforting message of the Gospel. They are flat on their backs and have no place to look but up!

In recent years studies have shown that people are most open to hearing the Gospel during times of major transition. These are days when people anxiously labor over major changes in their lives.

Such transition times offer rich opportunity for ministry, especially showing empathy and concern. Laypeople have a distinct advantage at these times because they have natural contacts with those with whom they work and live. Be ready to help during times of transition. (Paul J. Foust)

Specific Ideas Individuals Can Use to Reach Out

Family

Sharing Faith in the Family. How can I share my faith with my family? Several years ago my wife expressed a concern that while we were actively reaching out to the people of our community, we really needed to do the same in our family.

All of her sisters and their families were members of Christian churches, but we had never really sat down face-to-face to share our faith. Maybe our spontaneous expressions were enough, but why not try something more?

We had a custom of getting together for Christmas, Easter, and at a few other times. Why not plan something where we actually could sit down and talk frankly about our faith and express our love for our Savior and for each other?

Since all five families lived within a convenient distance, we decided to plan a monthly dinner together, and ask them to bring their Bibles along. We would follow dinner with a family Bible class. They all knew what was coming, so there were no surprises.

We started the venture at our home, and everyone showed up. While some of us had apprehensions about how everyone would respond, we started by suggesting that this was something we probably should have done before, and then we moved into an informal discussion of an easy portion

17

of the Scriptures. By the time we were 15 minutes into the process, our fears were at rest. The participation was great, the flow and involvement beautiful.

In fact, when the hour had passed, someone suggested, "Let's keep going." I urged that we quit while we were ahead and continue next month.

An additional and unexpected benefit came when one member of the family motioned to me to follow him into the family room. He wanted to talk privately. This was the best part of the evening, and it would never have happened were it not for the first hour of planned sharing! (Paul J. Foust)

Foreign Language/Cross-cultural

Foreign-Language Bibles. Give a copy of the Bible or a portion of the Bible to someone from another country, either when you are visiting that person's country or when he or she is visiting yours.

Foreign-Language Witnessing Materials. (See *The Evangel-Gram,* vol. 9, no. 4 [June 1988], p. 2.) Among the major sources for foreign-language witnessing materials are the American Bible Society, Bibles for the World, Concordia Gospel Outreach (tracts in 24 languages), Gospel Recordings, International Bible Society, Living Bibles International, International Lutheran Hour, Multi-language Media, and World Missionary Press. For more information, write to Sharon Poellot, 753 Buckley Road, St. Louis, MO 63125. *The Evangel-Gram* is a publication of the Board for Evangelism Services, The Lutheran Church—Missouri Synod, 1333 S. Kirkwood Road, St. Louis, MO 63122-7295, (314) 965-9000.

Lists of Foreign-Language Materials. Another excellent resource of more than one hundred pages, the Language Resource File, lists foreign-language materials including Scripture, tracts, booklets, and Bible excerpts in cassettes, braille, tracts, video, film, and books, along with addresses to obtain scriptural material in more than 500 languages.

Order the Language Resource File (LRF) from SCRIPNET, P.O. Box 7907, La Verne, CA 91750-7907, (714) 596-9328.

International Students. Many of the international students attending colleges and universities have never seen the inside of an American home. Call your local college or university and ask if they have international students. Then offer to host an international student in your home for an evening, a day, a weekend, or over a holiday (like Christmas or Easter).

Evangelization of Muslims. Between 2.7 million and 8 million Muslims now live in the United States, insuring that more American Christians will meet Muslims in the years ahead. In an article entitled "Persistence Key in Muslim Evangelism" (*United Evangelical Action* 49:4 [July–August 1990], pp. 8–9), author Georges M. Houssney offers four suggestions: first, show hospitality to Muslims; second, get involved in their lives; third, learn more about Islam; and fourth, pray. In order to learn more about Islam, attend a seminar by the Zwemer Institute of Muslim Studies, P.O. Box 365, Altadena, CA 91101 or Horizons, P.O. Box 18478, Boulder, CO 80308-8478. Concludes Houssney, "It is no secret that the Muslim world has closed the door to the Gospel. But God in his grace has now opened that door by bringing Muslims to us. It is both our privilege and our responsibility to reach out to them."

Invitation

Personal Invitation to Church. In his book *Marketing the Church,* popular Christian author and research specialist George Barna highlights a number of methods and formulas for bringing people into the church where they can hear the Gospel. According to Barna, "The most effective means of getting people to experience what a church has to offer is having someone they know who belongs to the church simply invite them to try it. Call it whatever you wish—word-of-mouth, personal invitation, friendship evangelism—this is indisputably the most effective means of increasing the church rolls."

Sports. Church consultant Lyle Schaller mentioned once that team sports are the single most successful method of introducing young adults to and integrating them into the church. Consequently, if you have team sports at your church, invite a friend who has no church home.

School. A child came home from school with a piece of paper on which were orderly rows of squares, some filled in with circles and others with Xs. When her mother asked about it, the girl explained, "These squares are the seats in my class. Those marked with an X go to church or Sunday school, and those with circles do not."

The curious mother asked, "How do you know whether they do or not?"

"That's easy," she replied. "I just ask them. And then I can invite them to our church."

Lifestyle (See Also Friendship Above)

Specific Nonreligious Ways to Make Friends with Non-Christian Neighbors. Friendships with non-Christians must be based on common interests, not all of which are specifically religious. Since some Christians don't know how to make friends with non-Christians except by inviting them to church activities, here are a few simple, nonthreatening ways:

1. When someone moves into the neighborhood, host an informal reception in your home so neighbors can meet the new resident.
2. Invite your neighbor to your home for a meal.
3. Ask your neighbor for help on a project requiring special skills or a second pair of hands.
4. When new neighbors are working outside, take time to chat with them. Don't be too busy to talk. Too many people are.
5. Hold a block party or a Christmas party.
6. Meet needs. Bring a dish of food when someone is hospitalized, shovel snow, pick up mail during vacations, etc.

7. Give a neighbor an article you have read recently about an area of interest or concern, e.g., how to cope with divorce or bereavement.
8. Hire neighborhood children to cut grass, baby-sit, paint, help haul firewood, etc.
9. Send Christmas cards. If you do, don't put them in the door. Spend the money for stamps. People love to get first-class mail. Don't you?
10. Watch the local paper for news items that mention your neighbors and give them your copy.

Patience. "The fruit of the Spirit is ... patience" (Gal. 5:22), even in evangelism.

Newspaper Events. Watch the newspaper for life events involving people in your community: births, deaths, graduations, new employment, promotions, etc. Send a thinking-of-you card, indicating that you remembered the person in prayer. As an option, include a local Dial-a-Prayer phone number. (Kent R. Hunter)

Show and Tell. While physical birth occurs nine months after conception, it can take considerably longer for a spiritual birth to occur—sometimes even years. Effective evangelism is a process, not a 10-minute event! Therefore, consider every positive influence and gesture that is extended toward a non-Christian as part of the witnessing and evangelism process.

Words are wonderful gifts from God. What we say is important, but nowhere near as important as who we are. It is essential, at the right time, to explain the plan of salvation when a person is ready to hear it. However, we have to be winsome to win some.

Who we are carries much more weight than what we say. If a person doesn't like me, my words are more likely than not to backfire. The fact is that I am the witness.

Before returning to His Father, Jesus said to His disciples that after they received the Holy Spirit they not only would receive power, but they would be His witnesses! He didn't say we would receive power to *do witnessing.* We would receive power to *be* His *witnesses* (Acts 1:8). My total life is a constant witness for Christ. I may or may not be an effective witness, but a witness I am, whether I want to be or not. So the issue is not so much how can I do witnessing better, but how can I be a more effective witness. The most effective communication is always "Show me, don't tell me."

Being effective witnesses will motivate us to become like Jesus Christ in every way possible. This is the most effective form of evangelism we can offer to the world. When it is said about today's Christians, "Behold how they love one another," then the words we say about our faith in Jesus Christ will carry great weight.

Squashing False Doctrine. You may be discouraging others from witnessing by the way you respond to what sound like their unorthodox ideas. Think about it. How do you respond in a Bible class or a private conversation, for example, when someone offers an opinion that you know to be doctrinally incorrect? Do you squash it or do you handle it tactfully? Do you say, "No, that's wrong," or do you say, "That's an interesting idea. Let me tell you what I think"?

When people squash the inaccurate comments of other Christians, albeit with good intentions, those other Christians may become more hesitant to speak about their beliefs to Christians or non-Christians. If I can't even express myself correctly in our Bible class (or private conversation with a friend), they may think, how can I possibly express myself correctly to a non-Christian?

Clothing Evangelism. Wear something that indicates your willingness to talk about your faith, that makes a faith statement, like a T-shirt or a thought-provoking or conversation-starter button. For instance, I once saw a little bronze pin that said, "Try God." I remember that before I became a Christian, occasionally I would have questions, but there weren't too many people around to answer them. Had people indicated by what they were wearing a willingness to discuss faith or religion, I would have asked them questions or would have been open to hear them express what faith meant to them. (Moishe Rosen)

Scandal Evangelism. In the light of the televangelist scandals, *Christianity Today* Senior Editor John N. Akers asks, "What will happen to evangelism?" In the past the attitudes of most non-Christians to the Gospel have ranged "from indifference to vague curiosity," writes Akers. Now the gamut of attitudes runs "from smug cynicism and suspicion to disillusionment and open antagonism."

Akers suggests three approaches to the question "What will happen to American evangelism in the future?" "First, we could remain oblivious to the changes, complacently doing business as usual—and becoming increasingly ineffective. Second, we could become intimidated and shell-shocked, abandoning evangelism altogether." However, he offers a third alternative: "We could rise to the challenge, reaffirming the biblical priority of evangelism, and discovering afresh our total dependence on the wisdom and power of the Holy Spirit in evangelism" (*Christianity Today,* September 2, 1988, p. 11).

Periodicals

Issues. Have *Issues* sent to your Jewish friends. *Issues* is an eight-page monthly, edited by Susan Perlman and published by Jews for Jesus, offering a Messianic Jewish perspective on Christianity. *Issues* is intended for thoughtful Jewish people who are open to considering the truth of Christianity. *Issues,* P.O. Box 11250, San Francisco, CA 94101-7250.

Waiting Time Digest. Leave a copy of *Waiting Time Digest* in the waiting room of your doctor, dentist, or hairdresser. *Waiting Time Digest* is a quarterly Christian witness tool, containing articles of general interest along with articles that offer Christian perspective and that portray the Christian faith. The publication includes tear-out postcards offering free home Bible studies in the basics of the Christian faith. To order, write to the Lutheran Evangelism Association (LEA),

P.O. Box 10021, Phoenix, AZ 85064, Erv Rasmussen, executive director.

Other Christian Periodicals. When you have finished reading the latest copy of your favorite Christian magazines and journals, (assuming they are appropriate for general consumption), leave them at your doctor's, dentist's or beautician's office for someone else. (Stephen Gaulke)

Prayer

Intercessory Prayer. Intercessory prayer is an essential part of our ministry for Christ. As people pray, God works. Evangelism with solid prayer backing has God's power. (Dick Innes)

Prayer for Inactives. Our Savior Lutheran Church, Burlington, Wisconsin, effectively used prayer in preparation for Every Member Sunday. Their goal was to have every member in worship on a designated Sunday, including all inactive members. Elders prayed, active members prayed for inactive members, the prayer chain prayed for six weeks, the congregation prayed in worship, and the members held a 24-hour prayer vigil. (Rob Bolling)

Sick, Shut-in, and Hospitalized

Witness in Rest Homes. Both Christians and non-Christians live in nursing homes and care facilities, often dangerously close to eternity, and neither has much opportunity to hear the Gospel. Thousands of these people are confined to bed, very lonely, and anxious to talk to anybody about anything!

The average Christian requires very little training to communicate those two great Bible truths of sin and grace. Walk into a rest home and ask permission to visit some of these lonesome people. These people will never add numbers to your church membership, but they may well be added to those who will be gathered with you in the eternal congregation in heaven. (Paul J. Foust)

Hospital Visits. When you visit someone in the hospital, close your visit with a prayer. If you ask the roommate if he or she would like to be included in the prayer, you will get a positive response quite often. Don't be afraid to ask. It may open up a witness opportunity for you.

Cards. Send get well cards and/or personal notes to people entering the hospital. This is especially possible in communities where (weekly) newspapers list those who enter the local hospital.

Enclose a card that conveys a greeting from your church, including a phone number and the name of your pastor. Invite the recipient to call your church to talk to someone about spiritual concerns or to request a visit. (Erwin J. Kolb)

Tracts, Tapes, Booklets, and Brochures

Tip Tracts. Leave a tip tract with the tip the next time you dine out. The American Tract Society offers one that begins, "Thank you expresses gratitude when someone does something for us. This card and tip, for instance, is (sic) my way of saying thanks for making my day brighter. Thank you also expresses my gratitude for the most important thing in my life. You see, God sent His Son ... " The tract goes on to share the Gospel.

To order tip tracts, write the American Tract Society, Box 462008, Garland, TX 75046, or the Canadian Tract Society, Box 203, Port Credit, Mississauga, ONT L5G 4L7.

Have a Good Day! With a circulation of 900,000, this four-page, $6 \times 6\frac{1}{2}$ inch message offers three pages of interesting information, quotations, humor, and trivia. The fourth shares a Christian message. Pages 1–3 catch attention, and page 4 delivers a Christian witness. HAGD is published by Tyndale House Publishers, Inc., P.O. Box 220, Wheaton, IL 60189.

Answer Booklet. The Bible League (listed under "Organizations" later in the book) offers a booklet for outreach to the community entitled "Answers to Live By." Subtitled

"Answers you can trust to some of life's most important questions," this 48-page booklet covers the following subjects: the Bible, God, the origin of the world, humanity's fall into sin, Jesus Christ, salvation, living as a Christian, prayer, marriage and the family, suffering and trials, things to come, and your own salvation. Keep a few handy. Leave them in offices and public places. This tract is also useful for churches and evangelism groups.

Cassette Tapes. Share a cassette tape of portions of the Bible with friends and relatives. Hosanna Ministries offers the entire gospel of Mark (NIV) on tape at little cost. The readings are of high quality and include some sound effects and background music. Contact Hosanna Ministries at 2421 Aztec Rd. NE, Albuquerque, NM 87107, (800) 545-6552.

Brochures. Order some of the finest brochures available on a variety of topics from ACTS International, 280 N. Benson, #5, Upland, CA 91786. Titles include "Conquering Fear," "When Things Go Wrong," "How·to Be Sure You're a Real Christian," "Overcoming Loneliness," "In Times of Sorrow," "Failure: Never Forever," "Winning Over Worry," and "The Art of Staying in Love."

Witness

Witness Covenant. A witness covenant provides Christians a proven way to overcome their fears about witnessing. Two or more people agree to meet regularly (perhaps weekly, perhaps monthly) to pray, study the Scriptures, learn, and grow in Christ with the goal of becoming effective witnesses. The witness covenant includes no pressure to witness nor a time limit within which the learner(s) must attempt to witness.

It does, however, stimulate a deep concern for the lost; a realization of the importance of witnessing, evangelism, and missions; a willingness to learn and grow; and a desire for God's Spirit, through personal renewal, to enable the person to overcome fears and become a (better) witness. It includes no calling program but asks participants to make a bold commitment to face their reservations about witnessing. Discussion is a major component of the covenant, as individuals share fears, situations where they have missed witness opportunities, insights from Scripture, etc.

Why a witness covenant? Simply this: some people witness effectively, while others are frightened about the idea. How do we get people from the second category to the first? A witness covenant offers one answer.

52 Suggestions for Witnessing. (1) Ask the Lord to guide you. (2) Ask Him to help you recognize what He's doing in your life. (3) Ask Him to loosen your tongue so you'll be able to talk about God in your life without embarrassment. (4) Let people see your joy in the Lord (not how good you are!). (5) Search the Word. How did Jesus win people? Peter? Paul? (6) Get into a Bible study group. (7) Volunteer to call on newcomers or radio and television referrals. (8) Invite a few friends for a weekly Bible study in your home. (9) Gather some neighborhood children for a Bible story hour. (10) Take evangelism training on a local, area, or national level. (11) Wear symbolic jewelry. (12) Let your home declare the glory of God: pictures, plaques, posters, banners—all can harmonize with your decor. (13) Use greeting cards with a Christ-centered message. (14) Use Christian art Christmas stamps. (15) Don't be a neatnik. Leave your church bulletin on the coffee table. (16) Put a bumper sticker or decal on your car that will identify you as a Christian connected with a Christian organization or cause. (17) Watch your neighborhood for newcomers. Be the first to call on them with a plate of cookies. (18) When you dine out, leave a tract along with a generous tip. (19) When paying bills, enclose a tract with each check.

(20) Consider whom you see frequently: (a) relatives; (b) friends; (c) neighbors; (d) fellow workers or classmates. (21) Look for clues to their spiritual life. (a) How do they spend Sunday mornings? (b) What pictures are on their walls? (c) What books are on their shelves? (d) Who are their friends? (e) What kind of music do they like? (f) What do

they do for fun? (g) How's their language? (h) How do they spend their money? (22) Asking God's guidance, make a list of those who seem to be outside the kingdom. (23) Pray for them. (24) Love them. (25) Seek their company. Invite them over for coffee (or appropriate beverage). (26) Ask God to prepare their hearts. (27) Ask God for (a) the opportunity to speak about spiritual things; (b) the discernment to recognize it; (c) the courage to speak; (d) the wisdom to say enough, but not too much. (28) Listen to them. Listen to them. Listen to them. (29) Watch for opportunities to let them tell you about their religious background. (30) Tell them yours, being sure to give God all the credit.

(31) Watch for opportunities to mention any or all of the following facts: (a) Heaven is God's gift. It is neither earned nor deserved. (b) All people are in rebellion against God. Therefore, they don't want to hear about Him. (c) For the same reason, all people are at variance with themselves and others. This is the basic reason for the mess the world is in. (d) Because God loves us, He must punish, just as a truly loving father must punish; but His overall aim is to bring us back to the joy of fellowship with Himself and of right relationships with others. (e) To this end He sent Christ. (32) Invite your witnessees to a regular or special church service, a Bible study group, a fellowship event, or the adult information class. (33) If children are involved, offer to bring them to Sunday school or vacation Bible school. (34) Try to arrange for prospects to meet other members of your church.

(35) Pray for these things for your church's evangelism effort: more callers, more guests, more people for the membership class, more time, more love. (36) Come to church at every opportunity (a) to recharge your spiritual batteries and (b) so you'll know what's going on and can talk about it. (37) Pray that the Holy Spirit will reach hearts through all of the participants in Sunday-morning activities: the pastor, the Sunday school teachers, the greeters, the ushers, the lay ministers, the coffee-time hostesses and hosts, the choir and other musicians, the guests, all worshipers. (38) If opportu-

nity offers, sit next to a person you do not know. (39) Be sure the person has a bulletin and a hymnal. (40) Help the person with the liturgy if the need is there. (41) Introduce yourself. (42) Ask one or two friendly questions, if need be. (43) Listen to the person. (44) Relax. (45) Give the person space; don't hover. (46) Try to learn (a) the person's name (ask for the correct spelling), (b) where the person lives, (c) how long the person has been in the area, (d) occupation, (e) place of occupation, (f) family, (g) church affiliation or lack of same, (h) how the person happened to come to your church. (47) Invite your new friend to stay for coffee and Bible class. (48) Apply points 20 through 33 as appropriate. (49) As soon after the conversation as possible, jot down everything you remember about your contact and give the information to your pastor or any member of the evangelism teams (unless the person turns out to be a charter member of your church!). (50) You'll be able to implement points 35 through 48 more effectively if you've taken care of most of your church business by phone or at other gatherings. If you have three documents to deliver, five people to see, and a five-minute meeting near the lectern to attend, you won't meet many visitors during the fellowship time. You may not even get any coffee! (51) Ask God to show you how much of your time, talents, and treasure He wants you to invest in direct church activities. After all, if we had no place to worship, services, Sunday school, choir, fellowship activities, etc., we'd have nothing to which to invite visitors. (52) Thank and praise God for opportunities to do all of the above. (Wenonah Deffner)

Part 2

Great Ideas for Churches and Evangelism Committees

General Concepts Churches Can Use to Reach Out

Attitude

A Strong Convictional Base. One indispensable foundation for any church and pastor is a convictional base, built not only on right theology but also on the belief that theology results in action. It is not enough to hold a conviction lightly. Evangelism needs the same bedrock conviction of a Martin Luther who is quoted as saying, "Here I stand, so help me God." (Win Arn)

Attitude Most Important. A compilation of data from 52 congregations across the United States and Canada identifies attitude as the most important factor in effective evangelistic outreach, according to author Hugo C. Kaeding, pastor of St. James, Quincy, Illinois.

Various comments from the churches underscore the importance of attitude. "Evangelism is not a program, it is an attitude." "It is not a particular program that matters, but an attitude." "Most important is the pastor's attitude. We talk about evangelism and searching for the lost in meetings, when talking to people, and in sermons from the pulpit." "This depends on the attitude." One congregation cites an "above-average attitude" due to strong lay leadership and a good pastor. Another sees evangelism as "just one part of the process." Another seeks to involve "the whole church in witnessing and not just a committee."

Why Most People Join One Church over Another. Research underscores why most people select one particular church instead of others. Good church location was 10th on a list of 16. The membership of a spouse was only 15th. The number one reason is a feeling of acceptance. Dr. David Jones, researcher in Jackson, Mississippi, says, "Persons are looking for a group of individuals who will first and foremost make them feel accepted" (*RD Digest,* January 1985). This number one reason sharply contrasts with the predominant reasons researchers found for why people attended church in the 1950s and early 1960s. At that time Americans attended church most often for the benefit of their children. In Jones' study, this reason was listed eighth.

"Process More Than Program." Such is the title of an article by Bradley G. Garrison, assistant pastor at St. Paul, Trenton, Michigan, in *The Evangel-Gram* (vol. 8, no. 3, p. 5). He reminds us that more important than program ideas are the attitudes that underlie the programs.

He writes, "At St. Paul we strive to communicate that every organization, every staff member, every individual is involved in evangelism no matter how they may be gifted. Our philosophy of ministry is that evangelism is the No. 1 priority of our church."

A Clearly Defined Purpose. *Refreshment,* newsletter of the Episcopal Center for Evangelism (cited in "Evangelism Newsletter"), carries the story of a pastor by the name of Neil Boese who decided to analyze growing churches to see if they could teach him something. He expected to find that they all had an aggressive pastor, good facilities, good music, meaningful worship, and strong youth work. None of these turned out to be the key factor in their growth. The one thing that all growing churches had in common was that *they had* *clearly defined their purpose.* They knew that their purpose was to grow spiritually and to reach out to the unchurched.

Principles

Why Have an Evangelism Committee? While an evangelism committee can actually retard the work of evangelism in a congregation, most committees help. Outreach is hampered only when members think that all of the evangelistic work will be done by the committee. The work moves forward when the committee involves members, communicates with the congregation, and provides variety in programming. The job of the committee is to plan, organize, and publicize evangelism, not to do all of the evangelism itself.

Make Visits. Every church needs some sort of a visitation program to contact those who visit services, newcomers to the community, and families that enroll in Sunday school, VBS, etc. Jesus said, "Go," not "Sit."

A Major Outreach Vehicle. Select some program, some process, some method for reaching out. Whether the program fits into the area of lifestyle evangelism (e.g., "The Master's Plan for Making Disciples"), visitation ("Evangelism Explosion"), correspondence courses ("Project Philip"), or home Bible studies (see Neighborhood Bible Studies listed under "Organizations" later in the book), pick a program and use it. For more information about programming than this book contains, read *Make Disciples* (Concordia, 1984) or contact your denominational headquarters or one or more of the organizations listed later in this book.

What to Look for in a Lay Leader Responsible for Outreach. Put a leader in charge of the church's outreach who has the gift of evangelism, the gift of organization, and a vision for the task.

Training in Friendship Evangelism. Train all members in friendship evangelism (also known as oikos evangelism, relational evangelism, or sometimes, lifestyle evangelism).

Use a tool such as "The Master's Plan for Making Disciples" (Church Growth, 1982) or *The Art of Sharing Your Faith* (Revell, 1991).

Put on High-Visibility Events. Plan activities that get the attention of the entire community, such as a Friendship Sunday at church, a sunrise Easter service at the ballpark, or any number of other activities.

Start New Groups. New groups often result in growth. Present groups can become saturated just like a sponge. For any more water to enter the sponge, some has to exit. The church that starts three to six new groups each year will reach out to many new people and solve the saturation problem.

Interactive Bible Study. Design Bible study offerings to give participants occasions to speak aloud about their understanding of God's Word and their personal experience of God's involvement in their lives (testimony), thereby enabling them to grow in confidence and in ability as witnesses to their Lord. (Ronald E. Meyer)

Interactive Small Groups. Design small group meetings (e.g., committees, organizations, classes) to give participants opportunity to talk about themselves in a small group setting or with one or two others. Give them opportunity to discuss God's involvement in their lives, thereby making it easier for them in other settings to talk about their faith. (Ronald E. Meyer)

Contact First-Time Visitors. When should a church contact first-time visitors and newcomers? Some say within 48 hours of their visit. Others encourage a contact within 36 hours, and others suggest a visit before the following Sunday.

Analyze the Worship Service. Does it flow? Have you eliminated lengthy dead spaces (not the sermon)? Can visitors understand and follow the service?

Define a Statement of Purpose. In this statement include a strong, biblical evangelism emphasis. Involve each board, committee, and organization in the development of the statement. Ask all groups in the church to discuss and adopt the statement and annually to measure their success in implementing the statement. Print your purpose statement in every bulletin, every newsletter, and most other church publications to keep it before the members of your church.

Plant a New Church. New churches usually reach out more effectively to non-Christians and the unchurched than established churches.

Specific Ideas Churches Can Use to Reach Out

Adult Class

A Helpful Notebook. "If someone should ask me, 'What for you is the most helpful book for evangelism?' " says Rev. Elmer E. Scheck, St. Peter-Immanuel, Milwaukee, Wisconsin, "my answer would be, 'Next to the Bible, *the most helpful book for me* is the little notebook which I always keep front and center in my top center desk drawer.' In this notebook I jot names, addresses, and phone numbers of everyone I plan to invite to my next adult membership class. Anyone who calls or comes into my office, who is not already affiliated with the church through confirmation, is asked, 'May I have your permission to invite you to my next class?' Almost without exception they give it, and I immediately put their name in the book.

"Two classes begin in January, Wednesday evenings and Saturday mornings, and two begin in September. Prior to the classes, those whose names are in the book get a written invitation and schedule, a phone call, and many times, a visit from one of our 'reachers.' We have been confirming between 40 and 50 adults a year."

An Invitation Process. Inviting people to the Bible information class is not a "one shot" effort as far as one church in Michigan is concerned. It is a well-planned process involving repeated communication with those who may be interested in attending the class. Seven weeks before the class begins, the prospect file is searched for names of people to invite. Six weeks—A personal letter of invitation goes to all prospects, and the weekly worship bulletin announces the upcoming class. Five weeks—A descriptive folder about the class is mailed to prospects; another announcement is placed in the bulletin. Members are recruited to serve as sponsors for prospect families. Four weeks—The pastor phones interested families. Oral announcement in church. Three weeks—Newspaper article. Church announcements and bulletin inserts. Two weeks—Training session for sponsors. Sponsors make phone contacts. More announcements. One week—Sponsors visit prospects' homes by appointment and offer to go to the class with prospects. The result in one instance—37 adults and 22 children were received into membership (*TELL,* Summer 1990).

Assimilation

Appoint an Assimilation Task Force. Many church members assume newcomers automatically feel the warmth and sense of belonging they feel. But, it doesn't always happen. In fact, if anything is automatic about the assimilation of new members, it's that they *won't* feel the warmth.

Churches must be proactive and intentional about welcoming new people into their family. A proven way to do this is to form an assimilation task force. This group (which should have a good representation of newcomers) takes responsibility for developing and overseeing a strategy of assimilating visitors and new members into the life of their church. Their specific tasks include facilitating new friendships, finding appropriate roles and tasks for newcomers, monitoring newcomers' worship attendance, and helping each person find a group that fits. One of the first steps of the task force is to interview new members (both active and inactive) and find out what issues they think should be addressed.

Canvassing

Visitation, Mail, and Telephone. "Bring new members into your church with Dataman's Outreach Management System." Dataman claims its outreach system provides an easy, cost effective, step-by-step approach to gaining new members. This system includes an outreach guidebook, sample letters, telephone tips, two sets of mailing labels of new homeowners, and cards for visitation and follow-up calls. The name and address and/or phone number are preprinted.

Dataman offers a four-step procedure, fully explained in the guidebook, that includes (1) visitation, (2) direct mail, (3) telephone follow-up, and (4) tracking the results. To learn more about Dataman's system, call (800) 523-7022 or write Dataman Group, 1140 Hammond Dr., Suite B-2140, Atlanta, GA 30328.

Sample Canvassing Forms. "The Community Canvass" is a 16-page booklet in a plastic ring-binder, containing 12 sample canvassing forms for a variety of situations. It also explains how to write your own survey form, offers record-keeping suggestions, and includes a brief bibliography listing other survey forms in copyrighted publications. Readers have permission to adapt or adopt one or more forms for congregational use. If you want to conduct a community canvass to help start a new church, to survey the needs of the community, or to discover the unchurched, you will appreciate "The Community Canvass." To order a copy, send $3.00 to *Evangelism*, 12800 N. Lake Shore Dr., Mequon, WI 53092.

Canvass Observers. Some Christian groups conduct neighborhood canvasses, going door-to-door to discover the unchurched and perhaps to witness to their Savior. However many Christians, intimidated by such activity, would never consider talking to strangers about their faith. Some of them, if invited, would go along as observers and prayer partners, if they were assured that they would never have to say a word. In this way they could discover that canvassing is easy, and they might be motivated to become involved more directly.

Church Consultation

Visit from a Consultant. Invite a church leader—evangelism executive, pastor of a growing church, a specially trained consultant—to visit your church, study your church, and make recommendations about the future of your church. One popular choice is Creative Consultation Services. Contact them at (800) 626-8515 or (219) 281-2452, or contact another trained church consultant.

Church Facilities

Well-Kept Facilities. Some years ago, when I became director of evangelism for about 350 churches in Michigan, one of the first requests for help in strengthening their evangelism ministry came from a congregation in a suburb of Detroit.

When I drove up to the church, the lawn was not mowed and the healthy crop of weeds made it look as if they had gone out of business. The church grounds had delivered a powerful message to me, the same one many unbelievers who drove by each day surely received.

The pastor asked, "What do you suggest we do to reach more people in our community?"

My answer came easily: "Call the trustees and get a crew of workers to clean up the lawn so it looks like you are open for business."

Congregations need to be reminded that there are two things that non-Christians observe about your church: (1) the outside of your buildings and grounds and (2) your people. Both leave either positive or negative impressions.

An old seminary professor once told his class, "The Gospel is dynamite! You cannot add any power to it, but you can sure mess it up!" Allow nothing to stand in the way of the Gospel.

Without question Christians themselves make the most consistent impressions on unbelievers and the unchurched, but surely the appearance of a church's facilities also plays a part in the outreach of the Gospel. What kind of a message are your church grounds and facilities delivering? (Paul J. Foust)

Parking. Start a L.O.V.E. club. That stands for Leave Our Vehicles Elsewhere. This would provide ample parking near the front door of the church for guests. Identify a L.O.V.E. lot. The L.O.V.E. lot is a designated area, furthest away from the door. People who belong to the L.O.V.E. club can drop off their family and walk. It is a ministry to the visitor and good exercise for members of the L.O.V.E. club! (Kent R. Hunter)

Church Structure

Leadership. Encourage your best qualified leaders to channel their time and energy into outreach to non-Christians rather than into leadership among Christians. Our tendency is to ask good leaders to focus on the internal affairs of the church. (Jerry White)

Ministry Manual. The Board of Evangelism of Lutheran Church of the Redeemer, Birmingham, Michigan, has prepared a 39-page Evangelism Ministry Manual. It includes the purpose and goals of the board, its scope of ministry, organization of the board, involvement of professional staff, and responsibilities of board members. There is a job description for the chairman, recording secretary, Gospel presenters coordinator, Gospel presenter, director of tract ministry, prospective members coordinator, canvasser, new members coordinator, new member sponsorship program director, new member sponsor, new residents coordinator, new resident visitor, visitor identification and follow-up coordinator, director of greeters, greeter, and special events and promotion coordinator.

Each job description includes a basic explanation of the position, a list of responsibilities, the accountability structure, an explanation of the position, the term of service, the approximate time commitment per week or month, and a listing of the spiritual gifts helpful for that position.

Copies of the manual are available for $4.00 to cover postage and materials. Make out checks to "Lutheran Church of the Redeemer," and mail your request to Mr. Cary M. Richert, Minister of Discipleship, Lutheran Church of the Redeemer, 1800 W. Maple Road, Birmingham, MI 48009.

Friendship Sunday

Planning Notebooks. Some readers are familiar with "Friend Day" and "Celebration of Friendship," two notebooks for conducting a friendship Sunday, respectively from Church Growth Institute and Church Growth, Monrovia, California. The Church Growth Institute also offers two other programs, "F.R.A.N.tastic Days" and "The Second Friend Day."

A follow-up to "Friend Day," "F.R.A.N.tastic Days" contains adult Bible class lessons, art work, audiocassettes, a Sunday school textbook for adults, a children's coloring book, suggested sermon outlines, a book about friendship that you can give to visitors on your Friend Day, a 30-minute VHS video ("Double Your Excitement on Friend Day"), a list of do's and don'ts, and a number of additional ideas. F.R.A.N. stands for *friends, relatives, associates,* and *neighbors.* The idea is that the church will plan four special Sundays, one on which to invite each of those four groups.

More than 30,000 churches have used "Friend Day" since it first appeared. Authors Elmer Towns and Larry Gilbert have incorporated the many ideas that have emerged over the years into "The Second Friend Day." You may return your order within 14 days if not satisfied. See "Organizations" for full addresses for Church Growth Institute and Church Growth, Monrovia, California.

Greeters

Lots of Greeters. "Appoint ten to twenty greeters (depending on the size of your church and number of visitors). When a young married couple visits, a young married couple will welcome them, and sit with them during worship. Following the service, they will introduce them to other young married couples and on Saturday will call to invite them back to church" (*The Win Arn Growth Report,* no. 14, p. 4).

Active Greeters. Trinity, Roselle, and St. Paul, Rockford (both in Illinois), have active greeters. They ask greeters to (1) arrive at least 20 minutes before worship, (2) encourage fellow members to be friendly to visitors, (3) make regular use of the guest register, and (4) follow up with a letter and/ or personal visit (*The Evangel-Gram,* vol. 7, no. 3, [March 1986]).

Greeters after Worship. One of the most important considerations in a first-time visitor's decision to return is the friendliness of the people. The assessment of that friendliness is most often made during the 10 minutes *following* the conclusion of the service. If newcomers feel welcomed and appreciated in this informal period of time, they will leave with the feeling that this church cares about them.

For this reason, a church does well to assign people who are specifically responsible for initiating conversations with newcomers and introducing them to friends. Greeters functioning after the service will actually benefit your church's welcome more than those who greet before the service. (W. Charles Arn)

Hosts, not Greeters. Drop the word *greeters,* and begin using *hosts* to describe those persons who formally extend your church's welcome. This name change implies, by the way, that newcomers are not "visitors" but "guests." Your "hosts" are responsible for "guests" from the time they arrive until the time they leave. This doesn't mean hosts must be with newcomers constantly. But like any good host, they are concerned that guests feel welcome, meet others, and enjoy the experience.

Increase the Number of People Who Say, "Welcome." Consider positioning hosts in the following places:

Parking lot: Responsibilities include helping persons find the main entrance, distributing a well-marked floor plan of the church and educational facilities, assisting parents with children, distributing umbrellas on rainy days, etc.

Portico: If your church has a place for unloading people in inclement weather or where attenders regularly unload before parking, several hosts should be stationed there.

Doors: Every door that people may enter should be hosted. The primary responsibility of these hosts is to identify persons who are new or visiting. The hosts should escort the guests to the welcome center and introduce them to the welcome-center hosts. (Therefore, you will need more than one host at each door.)

Welcome center: Most churches should designate a centrally located area of the church as a "welcome center." Put up an attractive sign and decorate the center. Welcome-center hosts should mingle nearby. When anyone (host or member) brings a visitor to the center, welcome-center hosts should be available to "adopt" the person(s) for the rest of their visit. The host(s) should offer to sit with the guests in the service, escort them and their children to an appropriate class, and introduce them to other members in the church before and after the service.

Classes: Every adult and children's class should have several hosts. Class hosts should watch for visitors, "adopt" them for the remainder of the class, introduce them to others, and sit with them. If the visitors have not been to the welcome center, class hosts should escort them there.

Literature

Attractive Brochures. While radio and TV offer stiff competition for communication in print, it will be a long time before the printed word becomes obsolete.

Effective Gospel literature can be handed out in person; distributed through the mail; placed in attractive display racks in doctor's, dentist's, and other waiting rooms; placed on counters at point of sale; used in prison and hospital visitation; sent home with Sunday school children; and distributed in innumerable other ways.

Like other forms of media, literature needs to be attractively produced with relevant topics that address the real issues of life. It also needs to be written in nonchurchy, practical, and realistic language. (Dick Innes)

Mailings

Junk Mail. Most of us complain about all the junk mail that we receive six days of every week. The reason we receive so much mail is very simple. It works! While direct mail may not be as effective as it was 25 years ago, it is still a very effective way to reach people.

The key to making the mail work, however, is the same as making any other media work. The message must have eye appeal and speak to the reader's needs. If it doesn't, it will not pass GO but end up in the trash.

Radio and television offer people many choices. If they don't like what is being said or sung, they switch channels. But every home has only one mailbox, and it may be the only way to get into millions of closed homes to people who otherwise may never hear the Gospel and who rarely, if ever, darken the door of a church.

The housing tract where I live in Southern California includes 160 homes. Twice every month another member from my church and I mail an attractive Gospel brochure (produced by ACTS International) to our 158 neighbors. Eighty families lived in my former neighborhood and I mailed them an attractive Gospel brochure every month for two years. As a result, 12 percent of my neighbors talked to me about these brochures and their content.

According to Lyle Schaller, author of 500 articles and more than 20 books, direct mail provides the most effective way to invite people from your community to church. It's better than the telephone which busy people see as an invasion of privacy, although the phone is excellent for reaching out to the lonely. (Your call may be the only one they receive.) (Dick Innes)

Tabloid Evangelism. Reach out to your community with an eight- to sixteen-page tabloid four, six, or nine times a year. Often you can find advertisers to cover most or all costs. Include articles of general interest and some information about your church on the front, middle, and back pages. Postage is paid at third-class rate for nonprofit publications. Contact Gospel Publishing Association, P.O. Box 94368, Birmingham, AL 35220, or call them at (205) 856-7070 for additional information.

Together. *Together*, an eight-page tabloid, similar to the Gospel Publishing Association's tabloid, now reaches 250,000 homes in the U.S. and Canada. Produced by the Mennonite Publishing House in Scottdale, Pennsylvania, *Together* looks very much like GPA's product. For information write to *Together,* Rt. 2, Box 656, Grottoes, VA 24441-9342.

Media

60-Second Spots. Today we live in a noncommunicative society. Once friendly neighborhoods, where people knew each other and spent time together in conversation and activity, now harbor strangers. No longer does news travel by word of mouth. It comes via radio and especially TV because families spend much of their time behind closed doors, sheltered from a hostile world.

Door-to-door vendors and visitors have almost become a thing of the past, except for a few brave souls, most of whom represent the cults. Instead, Christians now attempt to enter homes with the Gospel via radio and TV. Unfortunately, results have been limited in ratio to the costs and effort expended because mainly Christians tune in to Christian radio and television. We're mostly preaching to the choir.

As the old saying goes, "You don't catch fish in the bathtub!" If we're going to catch fish, we have to go where the fish are. The most effective (and intelligent) way to communicate the Gospel on radio and TV is to produce the right kind of 60-second spot messages and broadcast them on the stations and channels that non-Christians tune in.

The Mormons follow this strategy very effectively. Australian Christians had spots on almost 50 percent of the nation's commercial radio stations. Hundreds of people responded, and churches followed up with suitable literature.

In all effective communication, the secret is to "scratch people where they itch." That is, first address the needs that contemporary people feel. It is the only surefire way to open closed minds to listen to the Gospel that can heal human needs and hurts." (Dick Innes)

Spot Advertising. A Huntsville, Alabama, church has been using *television spot advertising* as part of its outreach. The congregation has received an award for excellence in local advertising production (*The Evangel-Gram,* vol. 8, no. 1 [September 1986]). For information contact Grace Lutheran Church, 3321 S. Memorial Parkway, Huntsville, AL 35801-5396, (205) 881-0552.

Local Newspaper. Before advertising your church in the local newspaper, you may want to write for LifeStream Evangelism's 13 readily adaptable newspaper ads. Contact LifeStream Evangelism, 7275 So. Broadway, Littleton, CO 80122.

The Episcopal Ad Project. This advertising project uses posters and $7'' \times 10''$ newspaper ads that are ready for publication in the local newspaper with a 65-line screen. Ads and posters can be altered inexpensively to become denominationally appropriate. The Episcopal Ad Project is located at 4201 Sheridan Ave. S., Minneapolis, MN 55410. Call them at (800) 331-9391 (in Minnesota, call 612-920-0658).

For example, one ad shows two children underneath the following headline: "Now that they know about Disneyland, isn't it time you told them about heaven?" Then in small print the words read, "Tinseling may be wonderful for a day, but heaven is forever. The _____ Church invites you and your children to grow with us in the faith, fellowship and eternal life of Jesus Christ." One of the posters contains a picture of the Ten Commandments on two tablets of stone under the inscription, "For fast, fast, fast relief take two tablets."

Prospect Newsletter. The Wisconsin Evangelical Lutheran Synod (WELS) offers its congregations a "Prospect Newsletter" service through its evangelism office. Subscribers receive 12 months of camera-ready, illustrated articles around which to build a monthly contact with unchurched prospects. The WELS evangelism office is located at 2929 North Mayfair Road, Milwaukee, WI 53222.

Films for Community Needs. Using a local school or meeting hall, many churches rent and show films for the entire community. Films from Focus on the Family, Family Films, and World Wide Pictures are especially suitable. For example, World Wide Pictures has released a four-part film series entitled Hope: *Hope for the Family, Hope for the Lonely, Hope for Forgiveness,* and *Hope for Commitment.* The films use dramatic segments drawn from selected World Wide Pictures productions. Write World Wide Pictures, Inc., 1201 Hennepin Ave., P.O. Box 59235, Minneapolis, MN 55459-9988.

The Bible on Cassette. Share a cassette tape of portions of the Bible with people in the community. Hosanna Ministries offers the entire gospel of Mark (NIV) on tape at little cost. The readings are of high quality and include some sound effects and background music. Write to Hosanna, 2421 Aztec Road NE, Albuquerque, NM 87107, (800) 545-6552.

Video-Based Outreach. Family Films (a division of Concordia Publishing House, 3558 S. Jefferson Avenue, St. Louis, MO 63118-3968) and the Board for Evangelism Services of The Lutheran Church—Missouri Synod have designed a video-based outreach program. Churches of every size and denomination can purchase a video package of 15 professionally produced Christian videos for children and supply them to a video rental store. The store then offers, rental free, a Christian video of choice along with the rental of a regular store-owned video. The church name appears on the video and on the free promotional posters. An individual, a youth group, a ladies organization, a church board or committee, or anyone else can participate. Call Family Films at (800) 325-2004 to get the program going at your church. You can request the program on a trial basis. The stock number for the program is 87-0863.

Video Training Tools. World Wide Pictures, the film ministry of the Billy Graham Evangelistic Association, offers three new video tools. *Billy Graham's Christian Life and Witness Course* helps Christians revitalize their own faith and share it with others. Lesson 1 covers "The Effective Christian Life." Lesson 2 deals with "The Victorious Christian Life." Lesson 3 discusses "The Christian Witness." And lesson 4 concludes with "Follow-Up." The tool comes with an 81-page workbook.

Witnessing Resources for Today's World covers in four lessons "Guilt," "Steps to Healing a Marriage," "Counseling People with AIDS," and "Sharing the Gospel with Jehovah's Witnesses." It too comes with a workbook.

The third video resource features Joni Eareckson Tada in *Blessings Out of Brokenness?* Four 50-minute videos explore these topics: "Why the Brokenness?" "Where Are the Blessings?" "Mending Things," and "Healing and Heaven." A compact discussion guide comes with the video. Call (800) 328-4318, or write to World Wide Pictures, Inc., 1201 Hennepin Ave., P.O. Box 59235, Minneapolis, MN 55459-9988.

Space in a Shopping Mall. Set up a closed-loop videotape with testimonies by individuals in your church whom God has blessed in specific ways. Place a tract rack or some brochures next to the VCR. (Kent R. Hunter)

Videotape of Your Church. In this day of visual literacy, you can present your best face to newcomers and prospective members. A five-to-eight minute, well-paced introduction to your church will show people the benefits they will receive from joining. You can also give a copy to members to share with their friends. Be sure that both the message and the production are of high quality; regular TV viewers expect it. (W. Charles Arn)

"Evangelism Tools for the '90s." This notebook by Harry H. Fowler shows pastors the need to examine past traditions, growth patterns, community growth, ministry styles, and outreach methods. It also explains how to use a variety of modern, creative ways to promote your church and reach your community for Christ. Write to Creative Growth Dynamics, Inc., P.O. Box 2095, Rocky Mount, NC 27802, (919) 977-1129.

"Public Relations for the Local Church." Church Growth Institute offers a notebook called "Public Relations for the Local Church." It shows how to develop a working relationship with local news media and how to create opportunities for positive publicity for the local church, often at no cost.

Written by Joel B. Curry, Director of Public Relations at Grace College and Grace Theological Seminary, Winona Lake, Indiana, this package includes instructions for using news releases, interviewing news media, designing and producing church newsletters, and advertising. Call (800) 553-GROW, or write to Church Growth Institute, P.O. Box 4404, Lynchburg, VA 24502.

Miscellaneous

Pastor the Unchurched. Where did we get the notion that only church members need a pastor? Compose a one page sheet using this headline: "Your Pastor, [name of your community]." Include copy such as this: "Everyone, at some time or another, needs a friend to talk to. If you ever have that need but not the friend ... if you ever feel like talking and need someone to listen—or maybe you need a ministry for a health or family situation—here's a pastor you can turn to."

Add additional (but brief) copy, written from *the reader's* perspective. Include a short description of yourself that highlights you (the pastor) as a real person. Then get out and knock on some doors. Introduce yourself as the pastor of "_____ Church." Explain that you're not asking people to join anything or give anything. Instead, you would like to be their pastor if they don't have one. Leave a copy of the one page sheet inviting them to call on you.

Also leave a brief questionnaire and a self-addressed, stamped envelope with your name (Rev. . . .) and address on it (omit the church name). Ask people to return it at their convenience. In the survey ask for information to help you effectively pastor the person or family.

Then, at least once each month, contact everyone who returns a questionnaire, using a phone call, visit, personal letter, gift, etc. Work on building a relationship, at their pace. You should be able to handle a prospect list of 30 to 40 persons.

Mix. An indispensable requirement for a church's outreach is finding its own mix—that combination of ingredients, in the right proportions, that produces effective evangelism. How does a church know it has found the right mix? When it works! When people become Christians.

What if your church's outreach isn't effective? Change the mix! Look at your church's prayer life, its training programs, its leadership, its spiritual foundation, its deployment of laity, its delivery of the Gospel, its investment of time and money into the evangelistic task. (Win Arn)

Neighbors Night. To build bridges to the families who live in the area around the church, especially those of different ethnic groups, try a Neighbors Night. First, plan a program that includes two speakers, a representative of the neighborhood (ethnic) group and a representative of the church. The representatives help the groups understand each other. Allow plenty of time for discussion. Second, provide tours of the facilities. Third, have plenty of refreshments and time for socializing. Fourth, provide a gift for each person to take home, an attractive picture or brochure of the church, a coffee mug, a glass, an imprinted pencil, etc. Fifth, provide a means of registration—with name tags—that allows you to get names and addresses. (Erwin J. Kolb)

Good-bye Ritual. To maintain church ties when people move, incorporate this ritual of departure into the worship service, prior to the benediction: "In God's plan for life we give thanks this day for (name or names), who have been part of our church family and who leave us and our location for a new home, new work, a new church, and a new life in (place or places).

(Addressing those who are leaving:) "Because we do not want your going to be a gradual fading from our lives and our minds, we joyously send you forth, with love, from our worship and fellowship. We give thanks for your time with us and ask God's blessings on your travels and future lives. Go now with our blessing and our love; go with God." (Ronald E. Meyer)

Printed Stickers. Put stickers with Bible verses on your letters, Christmas cards, packages, etc. They are available from Millennium Ministries, P.O. Box 1023, Lancaster, OH 43130. Call them at (614) 491-2930.

Hospitality Questionnaire. One of the best ways to build bridges to the unchurched is by practicing the gift of hospitality (1 Peter 4:9–10; Romans 12:13). Print the following hospitality questionnaire in your monthly newsletter, insert it into the weekend worship folders on a regular basis, or use your creative imagination to get it into people's hands.

Since many Christians have few or no non-Christian friends, we need to be intentional in making friends for Christ. Jesus shows us how to do it. He broke bread in the house of Zaccheaus (Luke 19:1–10), went to a party in the home of a

Pharisee (Luke 7:36–50), and took some criticism for associating with nonreligious people (Luke 15:1–2).

Please answer the following questions as a way of discovering if the Lord has given you the gift of hospitality and if you could use it to reach the unchurched. Your answers are for your eyes only.

1. How often do you have guests into your home for a meal?
2. How often in the past year have you had unchurched acquaintances into your home for a meal?
3. How often in the past six months have you had unchurched acquaintances into your home for a meal?
4. How often in the past month have you had unchurched acquaintances into your home for a meal?
5. If you answered any of the last three questions positively, did you discuss spiritual matters at all?
6. Do you see yourself as one who could make such an invitation in the future?   Yes   No
7. Would you consider inviting an unchurched person whom you already know to your home for a meal, a party, or an informal gathering of some type in the next three months?   Yes   No

Missions

Foreign Missions. If your church presently is not supporting missionaries abroad, the following ideas may help you get started. Write letters to missionaries. Conduct special offerings for one or several missionaries. Conduct various mission education activities. Post information about the missionaries you are supporting, etc. (Martin E. Lundi)

Sunday School Missions Curriculum. *Everyone, Everywhere* is a curriculum that brings the mission field to your students and helps them develop a heart for the lost. Help preschoolers through high schoolers explore their role as world Christians, understand missionary vocations and lifestyles, and investigate opportunities for full-time mission service. Write to Concordia Publishing House, 3558 S. Jefferson

Ave., St. Louis, MO 63118-3968, (800) 325-3040. (Paul E. Muench)

Bible Distribution. The following organizations, among others, send Bibles to other nations. If you wish to become involved in Bible distribution for world evangelization, please contact one or more of them directly.

- The Bible League, 16801 Van Dam Road, South Holland, IL 60473, (800) 334-7407
- Bibles for the World, P.O. Box 805, Wheaton, IL 60189, (800) 323-2609
- The Billy Graham Evangelistic Association, 1300 Harmon Place, Minneapolis, MN 55403, (612) 338-0500
- Campus Crusade for Christ, Arrowhead Springs, San Bernardino, CA 92414, (714) 886-5224
- Christian Broadcasting Network, CBN Center, Virginia Beach, VA 23463, (804) 424-7777
- Concordia Gospel Outreach, Box 201, St. Louis, MO 63166-0201, (314) 268-1363
- Gideons International, 2900 Lebanon Rd., Nashville, TN 37214, (615) 883-8533
- International Bible Society, P.O. Box 62970, Colorado Springs, CO 80962-2970, (800) 448-0456
- International Lutheran Laymen's League, 2185 Hampton Ave., St. Louis, MO 63139-2983, (314) 647-6923
- Living Bibles International, P.O. Box 725, Wheaton, IL 60189, (708) 510-9500
- Lutheran Bible Translators, P.O. Box 2050, Aurora, IL 60507-2050, (708) 897-0660, (800) 53-BIBLE
- Open Doors with Brother Andrew, P.O. Box 27001, Santa Ana, CA 92767, (714) 531-6000
- World Missionary Press, P.O. Box 120, New Paris, IN 46553, (219) 831-2111
- Wycliffe Bible Translators, P.O. Box 2727, Huntington Beach, CA 92647, (714) 536-9346

Newcomers

Get Lists of Newcomers. Four U.S. organizations provide information about new families moving into your area. The same information may possibly be obtained locally. Call or write one of the following organizations, indicating the zip codes for which you want newcomer information:

- COR Information, 117 Landmark Square, Virginia Beach, VA 23452-9850, (800) 877-5478
- GGC Associates, Inc., 2900 Bristol, Suite H-203, Costa Mesa, CA 92626-9926, (800) 444-9521, ext. 260
- The New Family Bureau, 2072 Northgate Dr., Columbus, IN 47201, (812) 372-1663
- Reaching the Newcomer, P.O. Box 640, Grapevine, TX 76051

Letter to Newcomers. Trinity Lutheran, Shamrock, Texas, includes the two Kennedy evangelism questions in a letter it sends to all new residents. Under the heading "What Else Do We Have to Offer You?" Trinity indicates the following two items in a list of six:

2. The proclaiming of the certainty of salvation so that you can with positive assurance be able to answer the following vital question:

IF YOU WERE TO DIE TODAY, WOULD YOU BE CERTAIN THAT YOU WOULD GO TO HEAVEN?

3. The proclaiming of the forgiveness of sins that Jesus Christ, God's Son, has earned for us through His suffering, death, and resurrection. God freely gives us His forgiveness; we have not in any way earned or deserved it. Therefore, you will be able to answer correctly and most confidently the following very important question:

IF YOU WERE TO DIE TODAY AND STAND BEFORE GOD AND HE WERE TO ASK YOU: "WHY SHOULD I LET YOU INTO MY HEAVEN?" WHAT WOULD YOU SAY?

Writes Pastor Andrew Simcak, Jr., "I believe that the inclusion of these two vital questions as well as their answers helps greatly to identify our church as a church that is concerned with that which is most important in life—our relationship with Jesus Christ."

Organizations

ACT (Artists in Christian Testimony). Founded in 1976, Artists in Christian Testimony (ACT) integrates artistic and oral communication of the Gospel into the ministry strategies of missions and the local church.

ACT consists of four departments—the Visual Arts Ministries Department, the Drama Ministries Department, Media in Missions, and Church Planting International. Through those four departments, ACT offers services to churches and mission organizations in church planting, worship and church growth, communication, integrated ministry, access to professional artists and designers, drama, and other areas. Contact Artists in Christian Testimony at 9521-A Business Center Dr., Cucamonga, CA 91730 (714) 987-3274, FAX (714) 944-7583.

ACTS International. ACTS (A Christian Teaching Service) mails Gospel literature to adults throughout Australia, New Zealand, and the United States. ACTS also distributes a monthly magazine, *Encounter,* throughout Australia and New Zealand. Dick Innes is founder and international director of ACTS International and the author of *I Hate Witnessing.*

ACTS' purpose is to help the church bridge the gap to the unchurched community through literature and through seminars on effective Christian communication (*I Hate Witnessing*) and interpersonal relationships (*Loving and Understanding People*). The ACTS Encounter brochures are most widely used.

Attractively produced, ACTS literature is based on the premise that arriving at Christian faith for most people is a process that takes time. ACTS literature is designed for continual sowing of the Gospel seed. For free samples of ACTS Encounter outreach brochures, write to ACTS International, 280 N. Benson #5, Upland, CA 91786, or call (800) 626-ACTS. In California call (714) 985-5350.

The Bible League. Formerly called the World Home Bible League, this organization has one clear goal: to place the Scriptures in the hands of men and women so that souls might be won for Jesus Christ. Its many resources include the marked New Testament called *The Greatest Is Love*; its Friendship Series; "The Miracle of Love" booklet for parents of newborns; and many English and foreign language Scripture portions, New Testaments, and Bibles.

Write to The Bible League, 16801 Van Dam Road, South Holland, IL 60473, or call (312) 331-2094 or (800) 334-7017. In Canada, write to The Canadian Bible League, Box 524, Station A, Weston, Ontario M9N 3N3.

The Billy Graham Evangelistic Association. Located at 1300 Harmon Place, Minneapolis, MN 55403, the Billy Graham Evangelistic Association (BGEA) has one goal, "to spread the Gospel by any and all means."

Most Christians appreciate the prime time respectability that Graham brings Christianity with his televised crusades, newspaper columns, books, films, radio programs, follow-up counseling, and relief efforts. The Billy Graham Center in Wheaton, Illinois, and the Billy Graham Training Center at The Cove in Asheville, North Carolina, train Christians for witnessing, evangelism, discipleship, and personal growth.

Center for Lutheran Church Growth and Mission. Located at Pacific Lutheran Theological Seminary (PLTS) in Berkeley, California, the center has the following purpose:

> To be a catalyst for defining and stimulating effective growth and mission in Lutheran congregations of the western United States. It will stimulate critical thinking, initiate research and development projects, promote communication among those engaged in

programs of proven effectiveness and provide motivation, study, training, and consultative services for seminary students and parish leadership.

Write to the center at Pacific Lutheran Theological Seminary, 2770 Marin Ave., Berkeley, CA 94708-1597, or call (415) 524-6746, FAX (415) 524-2804.

Christian Businessmen's Committee. The Christian Business Men's Committee (CBMC) has two goals: "To present Jesus Christ as Savior and Lord to business and professional men, and to develop Christian business and professional men to carry out the Great Commission."

Concentrating on lifestyle evangelism and discipleship, CBMC has copublished the video series Living Proof with the Navigators. For information about their materials or their conferences and retreats for business and professional men, write P.O. Box 3308, Chattanooga, TN 37404, (615) 698-4444.

Church Growth. Church Growth, led by Dr. Win Arn and Dr. W. Charles Arn, president, is the leading church growth organization in America. Church Growth publishes *The Win Arn Growth Report, Growth: A New Vision for the Sunday School, The Master's Plan for Making Disciples,* and numerous other books. Their church action kits include "Worship That Attracts and Holds the Unchurched," "Growing in Love," "Live Long & Love It!" "The Master's Plan for Making Disciples," and "A Shepherd's Guide to Caring and Keeping." Church Growth films include *For the Love of Pete, Who Cares about Love?* and *See You Sunday?* Church Growth also makes available the best resources from the Barna Research Group, The Fellowship, and Christian Business Men's Committee. Contact CG at 1921 S. Myrtle Ave., Monrovia, CA 91016, (800) 423-4844 or (818) 305-1280, FAX (818) 305-1286.

Church Growth Center. The Church Growth Center provides tools to help your church apply the biblical principles of evangelism and church growth; parish consultations; various books and cassette tapes; *Heart to Heart* lifestyle evangelism; and workshops. The Two-Year Church Growth Process works with a minimum of 25 congregations in a single geographical area, helping them develop the basic concepts of church growth through workshops and resources. The center also publishes *Global Church Growth* magazine.

Dr. Kent R. Hunter, Director of the Church Growth Center, has written *Foundations for Church Growth* (Leader, 1983), *Your Church Has Personality* (Abingdon, 1985), and *Moving the Church into Action* (Concordia, 1989). Write to the Church Growth Center, Corunna, IN 46730, (800) 626-8515, or in Indiana, (219) 281-2452.

Church Growth Institute. CGI offers 17 programs and four seminars, including "Team Ministry," "How to Reach the Baby Boomer," "154 Steps to Revitalize Your Sunday School and Keep Your Church Growing," and "Marketing for the Local Church." The primary seminar leader is Dr. Elmer Towns, Dean of the School of Religion at Liberty Baptist Theological Seminary in Lynchburg, Virginia, and author of more than 50 books. CGI's address is P.O. Box 4404, Waterlick Rd., Lynchburg, VA 24502, (804) 525-0022.

Evangelism Explosion III (EEIII). Evangelism Explosion III International, Inc., based at Coral Ridge Presbyterian Church, conducts evangelism clinics for laypeople in 121 nations, who speak 40 languages and represent 250 denominations. EEIII sponsors about 300 evangelism training clinics annually. Coral Ridge is located at 5554 N. Federal Hwy., Fort Lauderdale, FL 33308, (305) 772-0404, FAX (305) 772-0515.

Hosanna. One of the world's largest producers of the Bible on audiocassette tapes has served over 170,000 churches of all denominations, totaling four million families. Nearly 70 percent of the world's speaking population can be reached by Hosanna's cassette Bibles.

Over the last decade, as its primary calling, Hosanna has helped pastors assist their churches in learning about the Bible. Churches that have asked members to listen to the New

Testament once a month for three months have reported dramatic increases in all areas of personal and church growth.

Hosanna's tape lending library offers 4,000 teaching tapes from a variety of speakers. Other products and services include low-cost, high-quality blank tapes for church use; a tape duplicating service, with custom design graphics and packaging.

Throughout the world one out of every three adults, 15 and older, is illiterate, making Bible tapes an important outreach method. Write to Hosanna, 2421 Aztec Rd. NE, Albuquerque, NM 87107, or call (800) 545-6552.

Institute of Evangelism. For professional church workers, the Master of Arts in Evangelism is a 36-credit hour program that can be completed in 12 months of residential study after completing initial course work by extension. Core courses include history of evangelism, theology of evangelism, apologetics, and principles and methods of evangelism. Among many electives are evangelistic preaching, women in evangelism, and church planting.

The institute also holds several conferences each year, and offers continuing education courses on cassette tape. For information, write to the Institute of Evangelism, Billy Graham Center, Wheaton College, Wheaton, IL 60187, or call (708) 752-5904.

International Bible Society. The International Bible Society provides tens of millions of Bibles and Scripture portions annually, in English and in 350 foreign languages, using the New International Version.

Write to the International Bible Society, P.O. Box 62970, Colorado Springs, CO 80962-2970, (719) 528-1900. Its New York ministry is the New York Bible Society, 172 Lexington Ave., New York, NY 10016-7304, (212) 213-5454.

Jews for Jesus. Jews for Jesus (JFJ) has six permanent branches (New York City, Boston, Chicago, Toronto, Los Angeles, and San Francisco) and more than 50 chapters in other cities. JFJ also sends out mobile evangelistic teams and trains overseas missionaries in Jewish evangelism. Write or call for information about their media campaigns, cleverly produced broadsides (tracts), free monthly newsletter for Christians and another for Jewish people, Jewish evangelism seminars, Jewish Gospel music and drama, and films. Jews for Jesus, 60 Haight St., San Francisco, CA 94102-5895.

Luis Palau Evangelistic Association (LPEA). In addition to mass evangelism campaigns worldwide, the Luis Palau Evangelistic Association features a six-phase approach for mass evangelism, including Partners in Evangelism (a year before the campaign), Friendship Evangelism training, Counselor and Bridgebuilder training (for the campaign meetings), Nurture Group Leader training (for discipling new believers after the campaign), and Follow-up. The Luis Palau Evangelistic Association, P.O. Box 1173, Portland, OR 97207, (503) 643-0777, FAX (503) 643-6851, Telex 350076.

Ministry Resource Associates (M.R.A.). Ministry Resource Associates assists local churches to achieve meaningful goals through strategic selection and implementation of quality ministry tools. M.R.A. also helps churches develop the continuity, persistence, and accountability necessary for fruitful ministries.

Trained consultants work with churches for up to three years, to accomplish any or all of the following: diagnose the church's situation, set challenging, achievable goals, select quality resources, design implementation strategies, evaluate results, discuss difficulties, make midcourse adjustments, train lay leaders and participants, plan and assess congregational impact and involvement, and integrate sound principles of ministry and church growth.

Ministry Resource Associates also provides the following programs: Custom Outreach Planning, "The Master's Plan," Assimilating New Members, Family Enrichment, Small Group Ministry, and Mobilizing Laity. Write to M.R.A., 10209 S.E. Division, Suite 333, Portland, OR 97266, or call (503) 254-2424 or (503) 255-7690.

Neighborhood Bible Studies. Neighborhood Bible Studies (NBS) develops study guides for inductive Bible study and provides a proven strategy for reaching the unchurched based upon friendship and conversation. NBS study guides have been translated into 30 languages and are available along with seminars, workshops, and other materials. Write to Neighborhood Bible Studies, P.O. Box 222, Dobbs Ferry, NY 10522. Call them at (914) 693-3273.

The Oswald Hoffmann School of Christian Outreach. The Oswald Hoffmann School of Christian Outreach provides outreach training for college students preparing for professional ministries, for laypeople, and for professional church workers. It focuses on cross-cultural outreach and provides training in a wide variety of evangelism and personal witnessing techniques and methodologies.

OHSCO trains full-time church workers for evangelistic ministry, awarding a bachelor's degree to Directors of Christian Outreach. It also offers a Hispanic summer internship program, a Certificate of Evangelism Proficiency, a Workshop for Evangelistic Lutheran Laity, and other ministries.

For more information, write to Concordia College, OHSCO, Hamline and Marshall Avenues, St. Paul, MN 55104, (612) 641-8278.

The Petragram Group. The Petragram Group provides high-quality, affordable advertising for Christian churches, denominations, and ministries.

Purchase of a Petragram program includes an exclusive license for permanent use of all the materials in that program. Petragram's ad materials are ready to use and easily adapted for direct mailings, bulletins, posters, newspaper ads, radio spots, church logos, and other promotions.

Write The Petragram Group, P.O. Drawer 1877, Williamsburg, VA 23185-1877, or call (804) 220-1877 or (800) 634-8672.

Prison Fellowship. Prison Fellowship (PF) is an international, interdenominational ministry to prisoners, exprisoners, and their families.

Its in-prison ministry includes In-Prison Seminars, Bible studies, Impact Seminars, and Staying in Touch (a one-to-one visitation program). Its family ministry includes Angel Tree (a Christmas project for children and their incarcerated parents) and marriage seminars. After release from prison, exprisoners can participate in PF's mentoring program (a friend for the ex-prisoner), Philemon Fellowships (meetings with ex-prisoners and volunteers), Community Service Projects, and urban ministry (which works closely with urban churches).

Justice Fellowship, a subsidiary ministry of PF, proposes alternatives to incarceration based on principles of restitution, victim-offender reconciliation, and community involvement. Prison Fellowship International, the umbrella group to which PF belongs, holds consultative status (Category II) in the Economic and Social Council of the United Nations.

For more information, write or call Prison Fellowship, P.O. Box 17500, Washington, D.C. 20041-0500, (703) 478-0100; Justice Fellowship, P.O. Box 17181, Washington, D.C. 20041-0181, (703) 834-3650; or Prison Fellowship International, P.O. Box 17434, Washington, D.C. 20041, (703) 481-0000.

Search Ministries. Search Ministries offers seminars, conferences, small groups, and individual training to assist business and professional people to develop spiritually and have an impact in their sphere of influence. Search also consults with churches to help them effectively communicate with unchurched people.

Open Forum, the major evangelistic vehicle of Search, begins with a core group of believers who meet for three weeks to prepare for a series of four dinner or dessert discussions. During weeks 4–7, the core group invites friends for the dinners or desserts and prays for the entire event. Many guests leave the Open Forum having heard or understood the message of the Gospel for the first time. "Common

Ground," a monthly half-sheet of biblical instruction suitable for use as a bulletin insert, encourages Christians to develop areas of common interest with non-Christians. Search Ministries, Inc., is located at 5038 Dorsey Hall Dr., Ellicott City, MD 21042. Call (301) 740-5300.

Serve International. Serve International offers a six-stage evangelism training process focusing on the *Master,* His *mandate,* the *message* of the Gospel, and the *messenger, ministry,* and *mission.* This witness-building process mobilizes people for ministry in the local church and for world evangelization. Write to Serve International, P.O. Box 723846, Atlanta, GA 30339, (404) 952-3434.

World Vision International. World Vision meets the physical, emotional, social, and spiritual needs of millions of people around the world. Specifically its ministry falls into six categories: child and family assistance, emergency relief and rehabilitation, community development, evangelism, Christian leadership, and educating people about needs throughout the world (especially through the Missions Advanced Research and Communications Center [MARC]).

World Vision International is located at 919 W. Huntington Dr., Monrovia, CA 91016, (818) 303-8811. MARC publications can be ordered from the same address.

Program Materials

Programs from Church Growth Institute, P.O. Box 4404, Lynchburg, VA 24502-9985, or call (800) 553-GROW:

"Beyond Homecoming." This resource packet provides an outreach dimension to the annual homecomings that rural churches have celebrated for years. The target becomes the unchurched and those who have fallen away from the church (especially among members' families and friends).

The packet contains simple, step-by-step planning instructions, promotional material, suggested sermon outlines, a lesson/coloring book for children, and audiocassettes of sample sermons.

"Outreach 12." This resource packet by Elmer L. Towns provides a 12-week Sunday school campaign to increase Sunday school enrollment, particularly through networking evangelism. It includes tapes, lesson plans, student worksheets, transparency masters, posters for advertisements, and plans for ongoing activities. The program utilizes lessons from the 12 disciples on discipleship and relational evangelism.

"The Future of Sunday School and Church Growth." Dr. Elmer Towns, on VHS cassette tape, presents proven methods and principles to help church boards and key lay leaders develop growth strategies for the church. The program includes four 55-minute sessions, a companion workbook, a planning section, and a spiritual gifts test.

"How to Reach Your Friends for Christ." This program builds the confidence of average Christians that they are able to influence their friends to consider the claims of Christ. It was created to support and enhance a church-attendance campaign.

It contains five videocassette lessons (a total of 78 minutes) taught by Dr. Elmer Towns. Included are a teacher's introduction, an overview, a strategy for teaching, the five lessons with lesson sheets, and lesson plans and answers. Reproducible announcements, letters, bulletin inserts, prayer lists, and certificates help you promote the program. "How to Reach Your Friends for Christ" is available on a 14-day preview.

"How to Reach the Baby Boomer." Both a seminar and a videocassette and audiocassette resource packet, this kit provides the most up-to-date information available concerning the statistics, characteristics, and trends of this postwar generation. The leader's manual is intended for pastors and lay leaders, who, in turn, can use the student lessons to teach lay people. The video section features Dr. Elmer Towns.

Baby boomers make up nearly half of America's adult population and almost 55 percent of the labor force. If you are unable to attend one of Elmer Towns' seminars, consider bringing him to your church through the purchase of this packet.

"Outreach Bible Study." This video series, taught by Dr. Paul Cedar, equips laity to meet their friends and associates at a point of need or interest. The church learns a team approach that uses the various spiritual gifts of individual Christians. Order from The Beacon Bookstore, 901 E. 78th St., Minneapolis, MN 55420, (800) 444-2665.

Resources

Note: Resources other than those listed below appear under the topic headings of this book.

Evangelism. Subscribe to *Evangelism,* a 48-page quarterly devoted to "training Christians for personal witness and congregational outreach." Each issue introduces an outreach organization that could help you, reports news briefs on evangelistic events, and provides a fresh list of ideas for outreach. Specialty articles focus on assimilation, obstacles to evangelism, trends in American life, and conferences on evangelism. To subscribe, write *Evangelism,* 12800 N. Lake Shore Dr., Mequon, WI 53092.

Global Church Growth. Published by the Church Growth Center, *Global Church Growth* is the only worldwide missiological magazine dedicated exclusively to the Great Commission. It provides articles, resources, reports from church growth societies, and book reviews especially for those involved in the church growth movement, as well as stories about church growth around the world. To subscribe, write to *Global Church Growth,* Corunna, IN 46730, or call (800) 626-8515. In Indiana, call (219) 281-2452.

Growing Churches. The Sunday School Board of the Southern Baptist Convention publishes *Growing Churches,* a quarterly journal targeted to Southern Baptist churches, but with value for other denominations. It provides insights into leadership, growth stories from individual congregations of all sizes in various geographical locations, interviews with experienced church leaders, and an opinion about issues related to church growth. To subscribe, write to 127 Ninth Ave. North, Nashville, TN 38234, or call (800) 458-2772.

ELCA Resources. The Division for Congregational Life of the Evangelical Lutheran Church in America offers two resources. *A Resource for Leaders in Evangelism Ministry,* by Carl Shankweiler (36 pages, Augsburg Fortress), assists the evangelism committee in designing a program tailored to local needs. *How Your Congregation Can Become a More Hospitable Community,* by Gerald J. Hoffman (64 pages, Augsburg Fortress), guides congregations in practical steps to make themselves more open to visitors and strangers (*The Evangelizing Congregation,* Winter 1990, p. 3).

"Congregation Resources That Work." Purchase the latest edition of "Congregation Resources That Work" from Net Results Resource Center. Resources listed include those in the areas of advertising; assimilation; clergy leadership; conflict management; congregational vitality; evangelism planning, methods, and tools; evangelism study/discussion for groups; inactive members; large churches; lay leader training; midsize churches; preaching; small churches; spiritual growth; stewardship; Sunday school; worship; and youth. The resource guide also lists articles from *Net Results,* available as reprints, covering topics such as "Ethnic Evangelism," "Fellowship Evangelism," "Finding New Prospects," "Membership Classes," "Sunday School Evangelism," "Systematic Evangelism Programs," "Telephone Evangelism," "Theology and Motivation," "Visiting in Homes," and "Worship Visitor Evangelism." Write to Net Results Resource Center, 5001 Avenue N, Lubbock, TX 79412-2917, or call (800) 638-3463.

Lifestyle Evangelism Training. "Heart to Heart: Sharing Christ with a Friend" is a program that helps people learn how to share their faith in a natural way. Write to the Church Growth Center, Corunna, IN 46730. Or write to Church Growth, 1921 S. Myrtle Ave., Monrovia, CA 91016 for "The Master's Plan for Making Disciples," another lifestyle evangelism training program built around the book by the same title and the video *For the Love of Pete.*

"TEAM Evangelism." Church Growth Institute offers a kit called "TEAM Evangelism." Authored by Larry Gilbert, this lay-oriented evangelism strategy provides a place for everyone by combining the strengths of confrontational evangelism and lifestyle evangelism. The bold and confrontational evangelist and the meek and mild mercy-shower (and those in between) can work together.

Each kit contains a Lay Application Kit, a teachers manual, four audiocassettes, and an implementation manual. Contact Church Growth Institute at P.O. Box 4404, Lynchburg, VA 24502, (800) 553-GROW.

Book Series. Another resource from Church Growth Institute offers a series of books to help average Christians develop and use their God-given spiritual gifts. Gifts discussed include speaking gifts (evangelist, prophet, teacher, exhorter, and pastor-shepherd) and ministering gifts (pastor-shepherd, mercy-shower, server, giver, and administrator).

The first in the series, *How to Develop and Use the Gift of Evangelism,* helps Christians with the gift of evangelism to present the Gospel to anyone.

Attendance Campaign. From Church Growth Institute comes the attendance campaign "How to Reach Your Friends for Christ." This videocassette, accompanied by lesson sheets, helps you learn how to share your faith with your friends. It explains how average Christians can strengthen and deepen relationships with their friends and at the same time, share their faith with them without pressure or offense. It contains five lessons, a VHS videocassette, and a leaders guide.

These pages could list dozens, make that hundreds, of evangelism resources—books, workbooks, notebooks, resource packets, and videos. Some selections had to be made, especially for this section. These choices were based largely on quality, impact, and timeliness.

Rural Evangelism

Plats and Directories. "I've found an indispensable tool that not only helps me find where members of my rural parish live, but also where visitors and unchurched people live in the county," writes Rev. John M. Christensen of White Bear Lake, Minnesota. He is talking about the *Farm & Home Directory & Plat,* published annually by Farm & Home Publishers, Ltd., Belmond, Iowa 50421. It contains an alphabetical listing of every rural family in the county with mailing addresses and phone numbers and a plat and directory of every home in the county by township, making it a valuable asset for rural evangelism. The publisher can tell you if your county is available in such a directory.

Plat Book Evangelism. Christ Lutheran Church, Wolverton, Minnesota, made up largely of retired and active farmers, uses an outreach method known as "plat book evangelism." It involves three simple steps. (1) The pastor or an evangelism leader obtains a plat book from a member who has been in the area for a long time and knows the people of the area. Together they determine who lives on each farm listed in each section/township. (2) Next they determine new arrivals to existing farms. (3) Plans are made for members of the church to visit these new arrivals, invite them to church, and befriend them.

Steps to Growth. In "Fifteen Steps for Leading a Stable Rural Church off the Plateau," an article in *Growing Churches* (January–March 1991), published quarterly by the Sunday School Board of the Southern Baptist Convention, Gary E. Farley discusses how a pastor needs to work with the rural church. Among his many points are these: let the members of the church know about you; demonstrate genuine interest in your congregation's story; and identify the "bell cow" (leader) in the church.

Seasonal Events

Festival Outreach. Ron Armstrong of the Baptist Missionary Society in London writes about his days as a parish pastor. His congregation would distribute *10,000 topical leaflets* for the major Christian festivals (Christmas, Easter, Harvest) to invite neighbors to attend church on those occasions. "Americans could also include others, e.g., Reformation Sunday and Thanksgiving," writes Armstrong. "We went 'on the knocker,' as we say in Britain, i.e., house-to-house visiting. It paid off."

Halloween Outreach. Mission of Christ, an inner city Milwaukee church, hosted a Halloween party for youth ages three to sixteen, scheduling games, refreshments, and a movie. The party also featured a Christian clown ministry, Christian Halloween tracts, singing, and a closing devotion. Parents were invited to the closing devotion. Fliers inviting the neighborhood went out one week prior to the event. Some 150 children attended, and Mission of Christ members made follow-up visits on the families who sent children to the party.

Seasonal Inreach Evangelism. Christmas and Easter provide excellent times for churches to contact inactive members. During the weeks leading up to Christmas and Easter, contact them by phone, mail, or personally. If they worship, follow up with another visit, taking the opportunity to talk about the true meaning of that church festival.

Christmas Evangelism through the Christian Day School. The seventh- and eighth-graders of Immanuel, Mt. Clemens, Michigan, distributed 500 Christmas ornaments, brochures, and invitations to Immanuel's Christmas services. Members of Signal Hill Lutheran Church, Belleville, Illinois, mailed out hundreds of "Outreach Christmas Cards," inviting people in the community to attend their festival worship services (*The Evangel-Gram,* vol. 7, no. 2).

Parades. Many churches enter a float in a Thanksgiving, Christmas, or Easter parade. The message of the float provides the most obvious witness opportunity. Members of Redeemer Lutheran Church, Highland, Indiana, give out tracts instead of candy from their floats (*The Evangel-Gram*, vol. 8, no. 2 [December 1986]).

Holiday Visitors. What about those who visit your church during the holidays? Many churches use this opportunity to print a larger than usual bulletin, containing much information about activities of the church that might interest visitors.

Seminars and Workshops

Note: Seminars and workshops, other than those listed below, appear under the topic headings of this book.

"How to Break the 200 Barrier." This seminar, offered by the Charles E. Fuller Institute of Evangelism and Church Growth, helps churches move beyond the 75–150 church attendance figure. Some who attended have said, "This seminar has done more for me than any convention or conference in my years as a Christian!" "Being a layman, it gave me new respect and insight into the life and ministry of pastors." "This has been the most important educational experience I've had since seminary seven years ago." "The most practical 'how to' conference I have attended in years!"

What will you learn?

- How to develop the type of leadership and congregation needed to break the 50, 150, and 200 barriers
- The leadership differences between a "shepherd" and a "rancher"
- Common illnesses that prevent growth beyond 200
- How to plan for growth that avoids plateaus
- How to help unbelievers relate to your church
- How to mobilize your laity to break the 200 barrier
- How your group structure can open new channels for growth

The Fuller Institute also offers several one-day seminars: "Baby Boomers: Reaching the Unchurched," "Small Groups: A New Strategy," "Preaching to the Unchurched," and "Assimilation: Closing the Back Door."

Longer seminars include "Reach the Unchurched in the 1990s," "How to Have a Prayer Ministry," "How to Find Church Planters," "Basic Consulting Skills," "Growth beyond 400," "Beyond 800," "Strategies for Starting Churches," "Comprehensive Church Planting for the 1990s," "Drawing People in through 'Felt Need' Events," "Training Lay Leaders of Home Cell Groups," "Making Worship Celebrations Come Alive," and "Small Groups: Training Lay Pastors to Lead Home Groups." Write the Charles E. Fuller Institute of Evangelism and Church Growth, P.O. Box 90910, Pasadena, CA 91109-0910. Call them at (800) 999-9578, FAX (818) 795-9602.

"How to Diagnose & Renew Your Church." This three-day church leadership conference identifies the key indicators to the future health of your congregation, compares proven "growth ratios" with the ratios in your congregation, identifies the strengths of your congregation, and develops a ministry strategy appropriate for your congregation. For the place and date of a conference convenient for you, contact Church Growth, 1921 S. Myrtle Ave., Monrovia, CA 91016, (800) 423-4844 or (818) 305-1280.

Two Seminars from Church Growth Institute, P.O. Box 4404, Lynchburg, VA 24502, (804) 525-0022:

"10 Most Innovative Churches." This seminar shows churches how to update their programs to reach modern Americans with the Gospel.

"How to Reach the Baby Boomer." In this day-long seminar, Dr. Elmer Towns introduces baby boomers, how they think, why they lack loyalty to the church, and how you can change that. Towns covers the following topics, in this order: "Understanding the Boomer—Sociologically," "Understanding the Boomer—Psychologically," "How the Boomer Views the Church," "Principles to Reach the Boomer," "A Data-Driven, Bible-Based Strategy to Carry Out the Great Commission," "The Technologically Oriented Boomer Serves according to Spiritual Gifts," "The Boomer Wants Participatory Worship," "The Boomer Is Changing the Role of Pastoral Leadership," "The Boomer Wants a Functional Sunday School," and "Bonding the Boomer to the Local Church."

"Strengthen Your Church's Fitness to Witness." More than 1,000 churches have used the International Bible Society's evangelism seminar kit, "Strengthen Your Church's Fitness to Witness." It provides complete instructions for planning and leading the seminar, videocassette and audiocassette tapes, *Love Your Neighbor to Life* booklets, evangelism Scripture cards, reproducible masters for transparencies, promotional materials, and participants workbook pages. Each kit contains materials for 24 participants. Call (800) 524-1588. The booklet *Love Your Neighbor to Life* can be purchased separately.

Caring Evangelism. Stephen Ministries offers a 16-hour Caring Evangelism Workshop that immerses participants in a compassionate model for lifestyle evangelism. Write to Stephen Ministries, 8016 Dale, St. Louis, MO 63117-1449, or call (314) 645-5511 for a free brochure about the course.

Other Seminars Listed Elsewhere in This Book:

- "The Phone's for You"
- "Worship That Attracts and Holds the Unchurched"

Sports

Church Sports Teams. Many people love sports. Church teams often provide the kind of friendly atmosphere that makes softball or basketball great fun. Why not stipulate that at least a third of the team must be potential members of the church? This will create a positive witnessing atmosphere and remind the church that even though sports are fun, outreach is more important. (Paul E. Muench)

***Sports Spectrum* Magazine.** Tom Landry once said, "The star of athletic influence is shining brightly now." His words still ring true. *Sports Spectrum* capitalizes on that influence. This 32-page magazine is published six times a year by Discovery House Publishers, affiliated with Radio Bible

Class, a nondenominational Christian organization. It features articles about Christian athletes, color photos, columns, and editorial comments. Write to *Sports Spectrum* Subscriptions, Discovery House, Box 3566, Grand Rapids, MI 49501-3566, or call (800) 273-8333. Ask also about their radio program.

Sunday School

Sunday School Outings. I started teaching a Sunday school class of boys when I was 16. My most effective form of evangelism at that stage of my life was taking a personal interest in and being a friend to the kids in my classes. We got together for day trips and picnics. This kept them involved in the church where they continually heard the Gospel. Why are Boy Scouts and Girl Scouts among the very few organizations that stress outings? Why can't Sunday school classes, youth groups, and fellowship clubs take people on outings? (Dick Innes)

Target-Group Ministries

Target Groups. Frank Tillapaugh's book *Unleashing the Church* marked the beginning of a much-needed emphasis on target-group evangelism. Tillapaugh pastors Bear Valley Baptist Church in Denver, Colorado, a large church in a small facility with an emphasis on ministry to various target groups—mothers of preschoolers, seniors, international students, singles, street people, middle-class families, etc. Others call this ministering to people's felt needs.

The **Win Arn Growth Report** (no. 30) devoted an entire issue to "Target Group Evangelism—Unlocking a Secret to Growth in the '90s." After defining the subject, the *Growth Report* lists six steps to initiate target-group evangelism. In the same issue, Win Arn focuses on two target groups: (1) senior groups and (2) friends and relatives.

Baby Boomers. The "How to Reach the Baby Boomer" resource packet includes a seminar, a video, and an audio-cassette resource packet, detailing the most up-to-date information available concerning the statistics, characteristics, and trends of half of America's adult population. It also contains a leaders manual for pastors and lay leaders and lessons for laypeople. This packet is available from Church Growth Institute.

Christian Schools. Send scholarship gift certificates for your church's school to all families listed in the birth announcements in the newspaper. Send each child a Christian card and another scholarship gift certificate each consecutive year until he or she reaches school age. Many families may contact your church to learn about its school and its other ministries. (Kent R. Hunter)

Disaster. People facing disaster may be part of the ripest harvests. For example, some of the most hurting people are minority children living in urban inner cities with only one parent. Frequently troublemakers, they are hungry for love and attention. Christians who deliberately move in can reach out to these young people ahead of the gangs, pimps, and drug pushers. (Lyle W. Dorsett)

Senior Citizens. L.I.F.E. clubs for persons 55 years of age and older can help your church provide significant ministry to your senior adult members and also effectively reach out to older adults. L.I.F.E. clubs serve six purposes: to help older adults grow in their ability to model Christian love; to provide a supportive environment where older persons discover, develop, build, and apply spiritual resources to the issues they are facing during this chapter in their lives; to see friends, family, and associates of senior members come to faith and church membership; to provide Christian-oriented recreational and social experiences; to build supportive relationships among L.I.F.E. club members; and to provide opportunity for meaningful Christian service. Write to Church Growth, 2670 S. Myrtle Ave., Suite 201, Monrovia, CA 91016, (818) 447-2112.

Telephone

"The Phone's for You." Californian Norman Whan developed this program to enable people to plant a congregation by telephone (*The Evangel-Gram,* vol. 10, no 1).

One Michigan congregation made 18,800 phone calls; generated 1,950 names for its mailing list; and saw 150 attend its first worship service and 90 in regular attendance thereafter. Those figures substantiate the experience of other churches: make 20,000 telephone calls and you will have 2,000 people express interest in literature, 200 people will show up for the first service, and 100 will continue to worship. In *TELL* (Summer 1988), John Chworowsky lists six positive observations about "The Phone's for You" telephone survey:

1. It reaches a large number of people in a short period of time.
2. It can be conducted in any weather.
3. It is less intrusive than other personal surveys.
4. It contacts people in apartments, condominiums, and hard-to-reach homes.
5. It is easier to recruit phone-survey workers.
6. It is easier to train phone-survey workers.

The program is explained in a kit entitled "The Phone's for You," available from Friends Church, P.O. Box 1607, Whittier, CA 90609-1607, (818) 915-6611.

"Calling in Love." Church Growth, Monrovia, California, offers a telephone survey workbook, "Calling in Love," for use in established congregations.

Touching Your Community

Adopt-a-Highway. If your state has an adopt-a-highway program, urge a group at your church to adopt a section of highway and put its group name on the sign as a witness. Instead of its group name, it might put a short phrase on the adopt-a-highway sign, like JESUS LOVES YOU, FIRST CHURCH CARES, etc. (Kent R. Hunter)

Census Materials. Purchase census information about your church's community from CENSEARCH, Concordia University, 7400 Augusta St., River Forest, IL 60305, (312) 771-8300.

Church Facilities. Volunteer the church facilities for polling, blood drives, and other community service events to heighten the community's awareness of your concern. If your parking lot is empty during the week, consider offering it as a park-and-ride location. Then, on occasion, advertise a doughnut and coffee morning, and invite those using the parking lot inside to see the facilities. Place tracts and brochures near the doughnuts. (Robert A. Dargatz)

Demographic Analysis. Use a demographic analysis of your community to better understand the people you are trying to reach. Such an analysis includes data for three different mileage radii around your church, or you may instead request a customized printout based on zip codes or census tracts. A demographic analysis includes population, population by race, number of households, occupied units, average income by household, population by gender, population by age, marital status, households with children, population in school, working mothers, and housing units. You also receive guidelines to help you interpret your data and use it effectively and a computer-generated color map of your area with a five-year population growth projection.

To order, specify either three different mileage radii around your church (include a map of your location) or one of the following: three zip codes (additional sets of three cost more), three census tracts, or a map with a clearly drawn polygon inside which you desire demographic data. Order from Church Growth, Monrovia, California.

Involvement in the Community. Encourage Christians to be involved in secular organizations—the YMCA, PTA, curriculum committees, political action committees, blood

74

drives, local boards of education, Lions, Rotary, etc. Consider cutting the church schedule to encourage involvement in such organizations and in the lives of non-Christian people. (Jerry White)

Ministry Area Profile. The Ministry Area Profile from CIDS gives churches a better perspective on their communities. Using the most accurate and complete demographic information available, it creates a picture of the area surrounding your church. A free color InfoMap highlights population growth trends, and SNAPSHOT gives you a one-page graphic summary of your key data. Write to CIDS, 3001 Redhill Ave., Suite 2-220, Costa Mesa, CA 92626-9664, or call (800) 422-6277, FAX (714) 957-1924.

New Parents. Send a letter of congratulation from your church to all new parents in your area. In the letter, offer a free pair of booties for the new baby (or some other gift), available at the church any weekday. Give the names of those who respond to a group of young mothers in the church for a follow-up phone call, inviting this new family to participate in the church's ministry to young parents. Also use the phone call to obtain other information that might help the church build a closer relationship with the family. (W. Charles Arn)

Workplace Evangelism. Promote workplace evangelism by bringing together people of the same and similar occupations to discuss developing friendships. (Lyle W. Dorsett)

Visitation

Dialog Evangelism II. Dialog Evangelism II is an eight-week course for training laypeople in sharing their faith through a visitation program. Written by W. Leroy Biesenthal, it incorporates concepts of lifestyle and friendship evangelism. Contact the Board for Evangelism Services, The Lutheran Church—Missouri Synod, 1333 S. Kirkwood Road, St. Louis, MO 63122-7295, (314) 965-9000.

Dialog Evangelism Observers. The next time you organize trainers and trainees to make Dialog Evangelism calls, invite an observer to join each team. Some observers may eventually become trainees, especially those who don't realize they have the gift of an evangelist because they have never exercised the gift. Observing calls could help them discover their gift.

"Night of Caring." From Dynamic Communications comes "Night of Caring," a video-based program that trains laity to use one night a week to reach out in love to the church's visitors in a way that will bring them back to stay. The "Night of Caring" program focuses on meeting people at their point of need, concern, or interest, using a loving approach to visitation evangelism.

Dr. Paul Cedar, Guest Dean of the Billy Graham Schools of Evangelism, leads the 13 color videotaped sessions. The series includes two VHS videocassettes, a facilitators manual, and a students manual. Order from The Beacon Bookstore, 901 E. 78th St., Minneapolis, MN 55420, (800) 444-2665.

Prospect List. Here are 17 groups of people to add to your prospect list:

1. Unchurched friends, relatives, and business and school associates of current members
2. Family members of Sunday school students
3. Participants in special-interest groups that meet in the church
4. Persons influenced by special ministries, such as the aged, persons with disabilities, alcoholics, etc.
5. Visitors to worship services
6. People contacted through short-term ministries like vacation Bible school, day camps, or special programs
7. Participants in church-sponsored sports activities
8. Students at nearby colleges or universities
9. Persons responding to direct mailings
10. People who attend church-sponsored, high-visibility events, like seminars, concerts, flea markets, or neighborhood dinners

11. Referrals from hospital or funeral ministries
12. Neighbors identified through initial survey calling
13. Referrals from weddings and marriage counseling
14. New homeowners
15. Referrals from apartment managers
16. Residents of nearby group homes
17. Residents of nearby homes for the aged (Gordon E. Simmons, *The Evangelizing Congregation,* Winter 1990, p. 1)

Visit Other Churches. Visit other churches, including some of other denominations, to observe. What made you feel comfortable and welcome? What made you feel uncomfortable and unwelcome? What adjustments can you make at your own church in the light of these visits? (Robert A. Dargatz)

Visual Visitation. Two Wisconsin Evangelical Lutheran Synod pastors, Aderman and Witte, have developed a simplified 12-week approach to visitation evangelism, *The Simple Truth,* that uses a set of color graphics to illustrate the spoken presentation. In their preface they write, *"The Simple Truth* is designed to help remove the fear of witnessing and provide believers with an easily mastered method for sharing their Savior. It is . . . intended for novice evangelists, providing them with 'entry-level' learning experience." Callers use an attractive five-page, red and black flip-chart for the Gospel presentation. Only a small number of Bible passages need to be memorized. Order materials from Kremer Publications, 7203 W. Center St., Milwaukee, WI 53210.

Worship Guests

After Worship. After the benediction the pastor asks congregation members, before leaving their seats, to look around them, shake hands with people, and share names. In this way, guests receive a greeting, and members can give them a special welcome. (Erwin J. Kolb)

Chasing Away Guests. "10 Ways to Chase Away Guests":

1. *Camouflage:* If they can't find your church, they won't bother you. Don't place any newspaper or yellow-page ads, put up any signs, or conduct visible programs. Don't visit newcomers to your community.

2. *Long-distance parking:* Have your members take all the closest parking spots. That will make guests park a long way from the entrance and ensure that they won't visit again.

3. *Hidden doorways:* Since guests usually use the main door, members using side doors, back doors, and basement doors will be less likely to meet them.

4. *The cold shoulder:* If you do by chance see guests, ignore them.

5. *Hide the nursery:* In order to keep young families from joining your church, hide your nursery. Don't put up signs explaining how to find it. If you have one, don't staff it well. Locate your nursery quite a distance from the sanctuary.

6. *The old misdirection play:* Move Sunday school classrooms without announcing it. Use outdated signs. If you must prepare a chart explaining the location of classrooms, hang it in the janitor's closet. Above all, don't prepare a brochure for guests.

7. *Trash the restrooms:* Leave restrooms dirty. Don't supply them with soap, towels, and other necessities.

8. *The sore-thumb strategy:* Make guests stick out like a sore thumb. Embarrass them by having them stand up in church and introduce themselves. Have Sunday school teachers ask guests to read long passages of Scripture with names like Hazarshual, Meshobab, Beth-marcaboth, and Kiriath-jearim in them.

9. *Isolation:* If people do visit, don't return their visit. Don't telephone them or mail them any literature about your church.

10. *Leave it to the minister:* Remember that it's the minister's job to do all the evangelism. After all,

that's what you pay him for. You're just a layperson. (Paraphrased from material produced by International Bible Society, P.O. Box 62970, Colorado Springs, CO 80962)

Guests. Use the term *guests* instead of visitors in worship bulletins and for reserved parking places, name tags, and announcements. A warmer and more inviting word, *guest* suggests that members are hosts. Hosts have a responsibility to guests they may not feel toward visitors. (Ronald E. Meyer)

Letters to Guests. After people visit your church, write letters of welcome to each guest, individually addressed and personally signed.

Mailboxes for Guests. Churches that designate a "mailbox" or "pigeon hole" for every member or family for mail, bulletins, etc., can put a name on a mailbox, prior to next Sunday's worship, for each guest at church last Sunday. (Ronald E. Meyer)

Mugs for Guests. As a way to recognize guests in the worship service and to encourage members to greet them after the service, offer guests a free mug or coffee cup, imprinted with the church's logo and name. During announcements or whenever guests are welcomed, ushers come down the aisle carrying (baskets of) mugs. Encourage guests to raise their hands slightly so the ushers can give them mugs, and invite them to try out their mugs during the coffee fellowship after the service.

As people walk out of church carrying a mug, members can easily identify them, greet them, and get acquainted. (Erwin J. Kolb)

Name Tags. Plan an occasional "Name Tag Sunday" for both members and guests. Use a different kind of name tag for guests so that they can be easily identified. (Robert A. Dargatz)

Name Tags for Returning Guests. When members wear name tags, prepare two different kinds of special tags, one for first-time guests and another for those who have visited before. (Ronald E. Meyer)

Pictures. Post on a bulletin board Polaroid pictures of guests who visit frequently. This will help members get acquainted with them, promoting their assimilation. (Robert A. Dargatz)

Recognizing Guests. How do you recognize guests in your worship services? Some churches ask guests to stand or to raise their hands; others invite guests to visit the guest booth near an entrance, and still others rely on the friendliness of their members to welcome guests spontaneously. Few guests, however, want to stand in a worship service of 300 or more people, so members can't easily recognize guests. Ministers sometimes don't even want to ask for a show of hands.

Another way to recognize guests is to invite them to wear a lapel rose. Bright red and easily visible, lapel roses can be available (as a gift) in each pew. The lapel rose is available from Star Bible Publications, Inc., P.O. Box 181220, Fort Worth, TX 76118, (800) 433-7507.

"Visitors Don't Like Special Attention." This is according to a survey by the Barna Research Group. In "Never on a Sunday: The Challenge of the Unchurched," the Glendale, California, research group shares the results of surveys of more than 900 unchurched adults nationwide, asking for their reactions to nine different ways churches treat newcomers. Of those surveyed, 47 percent said they would "dislike a lot" being identified during the service to let members know where they were sitting, and 43 percent said the same about wearing name tags. Another 34 percent indicated the same response to having the pastor or someone else from the church visit in their home.

A total 74 percent indicated they would like to find out more about the church they were visiting, but in ways that do not draw attention to them. Thirty-eight percent said they would "like a lot" printed information from ushers about the church; 37 percent indicated the same response to receiving a thank-you letter from the pastor after their visit; and 33 percent said they would like it if "the church did nothing special for visitors; treated them like members." Thirty percent said they would "like a lot" members of the church greeting them individually, and 37 percent said they would like it "a little."

George Barna, president of the Barna Research Group, said that methods that draw attention to visitors often put the spotlight on people who, at least at first, would rather remain anonymous.

"Many unchurched people are uncomfortable returning to church," Barna explained. "They don't know anyone in the congregation; they don't know the traditions of the church; they're often not sure what to expect next in the service; and then suddenly they become the focus of the entire congregation."

Barna added that many unchurched visitors are interested in getting to know people and want more information about the church, but they want to do so in their own time and on their own terms. They don't want to be thrust into a situation they perceive as threatening or embarrassing.

The report notes that "visiting a church is a relatively uncomfortable experience for many people—especially those who have been outside the mainstream of church life for a time, and are cautiously considering whether or not to start attending. Tactics which put the visitor on the spot, however well intentioned, are likely to cause more harm than benefit" (*Reporter/Alive,* vol. 17, no. 7 [March 11, 1991], p. 3).

Take Guests Home. Recruit hosts who are willing to invite worship guests to their home, soon after their initial contact with the congregation, for a brief social time. (Ronald E. Meyer)

36 Hours. Through research one U.S. denomination has discovered the "36-hour principle." This principle states that when laypersons visit the home of a first-time worshiper within 36 hours, 85 percent of these worshipers will return to worship the next Sunday.

Worship Practices

"**Light Lines.**" *Net Results,* a monthly evangelism resource from the National Evangelistic Association, includes "Light Lines," a photo-reproducible "worship bulletin insert designed to raise consciousness regarding the need for evangelism and to encourage members to invite people to attend worship."

Congregations that subscribe to *Net Results* have permission to reproduce as many copies of "Light Lines" for bulletin inserts as they need but may not use it in newsletters or share it with other congregations.

Besides the bulletin insert, *Net Results* includes a regular article by Lyle Schaller and first-person accounts from several congregations about ideas that they have used.

The publisher is the evangelism arm of the Christian Church (Disciples of Christ). Cooperating in the publication are the evangelism departments of the United Methodist Church, the American Baptist Churches, Presbyterian Church (USA), and the Christian Reformed Church. For information, call (800) 638-3463 or write Net Results Resource Center, 5001 Avenue N, Lubbock, TX 79412-2917.

"**Who's Being Overlooked?**" This bulletin insert urges readers to become more conscious of other people with whom to share the Gospel. Free in quantities to members of the ELCA for a small handling charge, others can write for item number 67-3139 to the ELCA Distribution Service, 426 South Fifth St., Box 1209, Minneapolis, MN 55440.

"**Common Ground.**" This monthly bulletin insert from Search Ministries, offers biblical instruction on how to effectively share the good news with non-Christians in a natural and relaxed way. The insert encourages Christians to develop areas of common interest with non-Christians. Write to Search

Ministries, Inc., 5038 Dorsey Hall Dr., Ellicott City, MD 21042, or call (301) 740-5300.

Add a New Worship Service. Approximately 80 percent of all churches that add a new service will experience growth because more choices and more options will appeal to more people. Base the new service on research that identifies (1) your "target group," (2) the best style of service for that group, and (3) the best time and place for the service. Promote your alternative service well among prospective participants. Inactive members are often good candidates as well. (W. Charles Arn)

"How to Go to Two Services." This resource packet shows churches with one Sunday service how to add a second. It contains a two-hour VHS video, notes to aid viewing, surveys and questionnaires for gathering data, an in-depth explanatory text, and promotional pieces (announcements, letters, newspaper ad, and a telephone script).

Writes Elmer Towns, "Most churches want additional auditorium space and parking without the expense [of] building a larger sanctuary. . . . Some begin a second service as a convenience to worshipers, while still others want to provide different forms of worship. Probably the greatest reason is to turn the church into a multiple-cell church so each service is a source of ministry and growth."

Because of the move to two services, one church in Homer, New York grew from an average attendance of 325 in 1987 to an average of 435 in 1988. The initial growth took place almost overnight and has continued.

The packet contains a weekly checklist of steps that lead to two services. It provides survey forms for interviewing people in the congregation, on the board, and from other churches. A second survey monitors your success after the move to a second service. The videotape shows different groups in the church the necessity of the second service and explains how to implement it. For information or to request a 14-day preview of the program, contact the Church Growth Institute.

Worship and Outreach. The connection between worship and outreach is biblical (e.g., 1 Cor. 14:23–25) and crucial if church members are going to develop outreach attitudes. That church where worship is comprehensible to the potential Christian as well as the Christian will more effectively cultivate a love for the lost. (Paul E. Muench)

Outreach *in* Worship. Set aside time in some worship services for the following:

1. Silent prayer for the lost in general and for individual acquaintances
2. Worshipers to share in writing (on specially prepared forms) names and addresses of people they know for whom they desire the congregation's ministry
3. Worshipers to contemplate the purpose of their church

"Worship That Attracts and Holds the Unchurched." In this one-day (five-hour) leadership seminar for pastors, staff, and worship leaders, seminar leader Robert Orr covers numerous topics:

- Why Americans Do and Don't Go to Church
- 10 Characteristics of Churches Reaching People Today
- Planning and Evaluating Your Worship
- Reaching Newcomers While Keeping Old Timers
- Increasing Worship Attendance Frequency of Your Present Members
- Determining How Many Visitors You Need to Grow
- How to Attract Visitors
- Successful Visitor Follow-up
- Starting a New Worship Service
- Characteristics of Worship Services That Attract the Unchurched

"Worship That Attracts and Holds the Unchurched" is available on videocassette tapes with accompanying workbook from Church Growth, 1921 S. Myrtle Ave., Monrovia, CA, 91016, (800) 423-4844 or (818) 305-1280.

"Making Worship Celebrations Come Alive." This seminar from the Charles E. Fuller Institute (P.O. Box 91990, Pasadena, CA 91109-1990) looks at the worship service as a tool for church growth. Presented by Carl George, it covers the human need for celebration and pageantry, the role of prayer in planning worship, and the role of art forms in worship. It also addresses preevangelism and seeker-friendly services within the framework of your worship tradition, identifies trends in Saturday night services and children's ministries, and shares case studies of emerging models of celebrative worship. For current dates and locations, call (800) 339-9564 in California or (800) 221-9479 outside California.

"Six Ways to Increase Your Worship Attendance." This article from *The Win Arn Growth Report,* number 29, explains how to monitor attendance and respond to signs of inactivity, ask members to set goals for worship attendance, make worship services into celebrations, involve more people in worship roles and ministries, obtain feedback from members on important issues in their lives, and expand the number and variety of services.

According to this article, "A national opinion poll" shows that "a common attitude of the average unchurched American about Sunday church service is that 'it's boring and irrelevant.' Yet churches growing through 'conversion growth' have learned how to provide meaningful, attractive worship." For more information about the six ways to increase worship attendance, contact Church Growth, 1921 S. Myrtle Ave., Monrovia, CA, 91016, (800) 423-4844 or (818) 305-1280.

Invitational Worship. This 90-minute, six-part video series from The Fellowship Ministries helps churches make their worship more open to guests. Hosted by Rev. Gene Wagner, Grace Lutheran, Huntsville, Alabama, the series includes leaders and discussion guides written by Rev. Bruce Biesenthal, Peace Lutheran, Lombard, Illinois. Use this video series for adult education forums; for worship, music, and evangelism committees; and for professional church workers discussion groups.

Entertainment Evangelism. This video resource defines entertainment as (1) the act of showing hospitality, (2) the act of receiving and caring for guests, and (3) the act of catching and holding attention for an extended period. Rev. Walt Kallestad, pastor of Community Church of Joy, Glendale, Arizona, a church that has grown from 200 to 5,000 in 10 years, helps you analyze your church's worship: Is your worship hospitable? Do you receive and care for guests? Does your worship hold people's attention?

Contact Church Growth, 1921 S. Myrtle Ave., Monrovia, CA 91016, (800) 423-4844 or (818) 305-1280.

New Music Styles. Throughout history the church has set the Word of God to music, at times taking the lead in developing or enlarging music styles (e.g., J. S. Bach, African American Gospel music). Let's encourage Christians to write new songs for the church. (Paul E. Muench)

Contributors

W. Charles Arn
1921 S. Myrtle Ave.
Monrovia, CA 91016
(818) 305-1280

Win Arn
1921 S. Myrtle Ave.
Monrovia, CA 91016
(818) 305-1280

Rob Bolling
417 S. Kane St.
Burlington, WI 53105

Robert A. Dargatz
1530 Concordia
Irvine, CA 92715-3299

Wenonah Deffner
110 N. Gammon Rd.
Madison, WI 53717-1301

Lyle W. Dorsett
702 N. Howard
Wheaton, IL 60187

Paul J. Foust
1538 York Terrace
Saline, MI 48176

Stephen E. Gaulke
223 W. Sixth St.
Hazleton, PA 18201-4250

Kent R. Hunter
Church Growth Center
Corunna, IN 46730

Dick Innes
280 N. Benson, #5
Upland, CA 91786

Erwin J. Kolb
12429 Matthews Lane
St. Louis, MO 63127

Martin E. Lundi
4150 Goodlette Rd. North
Naples, FL 33940

Ronald E. Meyer
8100 W. Capitol Dr.
Milwaukee, WI 53222

Paul E. Muench
303 N. Lake St.
Aurora, IL 60507-2050

Moishe Rosen
Jews for Jesus
60 Haight St.
San Francisco, CA 94102-5895

Jerry White
The Navigators
P.O. Box 6000
Colorado Springs, CO 80934

Index

Items in this index are arranged alphabetically by subtitles in the text and also by some additional terms.